ALMOST
SHATTERED

ONE WOMAN'S COURAGEOUS JOURNEY THROUGH
LOVE, LOSS, AND LIES

KRISTINA WILDS

Printed in the United States of America
First Printing, 2018

ISBN: 978-0-9980752-3-5 (Paperback)
      978-0-9980752-4-2 (Hardcover)

Published by Book Counselor, LLC
Bookcounselor.com

THE
BOOK
COUNSELOR

Contents

Introduction

Sometimes we get so caught up in our everyday routines, we miss the obvious. My husband was changing. He was withering right in front of my eyes, a little bit each day. Maybe I didn't want to see it? Maybe my denial of the truth smacking me in the face was so painful, I buried it somewhere in my subconscious. Or maybe the reality of my life was so stark, I chose not to face it. Whatever I was doing, it delayed the pain for a moment. Pain procrastination is all I could do to survive the situation. Eventually, reality catches you, and when it does, we have no choice but to look it square in the eyes. It is in that moment of face-to-face, eye-to-eye engagement that a decision must be made. Will you battle, or will you faint? I chose to fight with everything I had in me.

Let me ask you, have you ever felt so desperate, so lonely, so terrified you weren't sure you would make it through? Have you ever been so consumed with rage and hurt it caused an actual physical ache? If you have experienced loss, betrayal or abandonment, this book will bring you hope. We never know our own strength and capabilities until we are tested. I was tested, over and over again. When my husband died, my life changed forever. In the hours and moments that followed his death, I experienced a sadness so profound I had to share my story. I also experienced a joy and thankfulness I have never felt before. My gratitude for the people who showed up for me during that dark time is immense. My friends carried me to a safe harbor. This book is dedicated to every one of my friends who brought me food, showed up to chat, watched my child, bought me groceries and simply listened when I needed to vent. I am forever grateful. You know who you are, each and every one of you! Thank you, I am blessed.

CHAPTER 1

Turbulence

I thought I was going to die. My hands were shaking, a cold sweat covered me like a blanket, and I could feel my heart pounding in my chest. I didn't want my life to end in a fiery explosion of flesh and metal. There was no one to grab for a final embrace, no last "I love you, man," just me, alone and terrified. I gripped the arm rests of my seat, prayed, and hung on.

Turbulence normally didn't bother me because I'd been flying since I was two years old. This was different. The captain came over the loudspeaker and said, "Flight attendants, take your seats. Ladies and gentlemen, I apologize, we have encountered some unexpected air pockets, and we've got some serious turbulence ahead."

He wasn't exaggerating. As the plane bounced and tossed like a runaway roller coaster, people all around me gasped and shrieked. Even the flight attendants couldn't conceal their fear.

We were flying from Washington, DC, to Denver. I had gone to visit my best friend, Jill, in Washington, DC, and was headed back home to Albuquerque, New Mexico, with a quick stop in Denver. I was one of the first people on the plane because I'm always punctual. I was wearing a pair of my favorite jeans, platform, red shiny boots that made me look 6 feet tall, and two items that my sister gave me—a vintage, black leather jacket and a knit top with sewn-in glitter. Needless to say, I was conspicuous.

As the turbulence continued and worsened, my first thought if we crashed was how they would find my body clad in this ridiculous outfit. I love fashion and was a slave to it in some ways, but this ensemble was over the top!

Then it occurred to me, "Holy crap. How could this be happening to me now when my life is so in order? I'm right with God. I'm right with my job (I teach piano and have over 60 students). I have a quaint little house. I'm single and enjoying it and not desperate for a partner. My life is finally looking up, and it's all going to end in a fiery heap of smoke and debris. I'm going to heaven; this is finally it!"

There was a lot of noise as the plane tossed and turned. Then we heard a bang–it sounded like a shotgun going off, only louder. It was so disturbing that I leaned over to the gentleman sitting in the aisle seat across from me and asked, "Excuse me. Are we going to die?"

His reply was perfect. "Eventually, but probably not today," he said. Relief swept over me like a cool breeze. His steady voice and self-assured manner calmed me down almost instantly.

Turbulence

Before the turbulence hit and consumed me with fear, I was reading a book called *The Secret*, which basically showed that we can create what we desire because our thoughts are so powerful. If we can see it, we can be it. I thought, "Gosh, this is so cool. I'm going to create my soul mate. I'm going to use the power of my thoughts to create the ideal guy, and he's going to walk into my life and sweep me off my feet!"

Well, little did I know it at the time, this relatively nondescript, vanilla, straight-laced, average-sized man sitting across from me, Steve Williams, would later become my husband. He had all the qualities that I wanted in a soul mate, expect one (he wasn't terribly tall).

It wasn't love at first sight by any means. When he first entered the plane, I thought, "He's kind of okay-looking. He appears to be a nice guy," but I wasn't attracted to him, and I certainly didn't have that leap in my chest or quickening of the pulse like you have when you see someone you find physically attractive. He seemed like a pleasant, safe, steady guy who was comfortable in his own skin.

Early in the flight, I also noticed that he ordered a beer and a glass of merlot. Who does that? I thought, "Oh, wow, stay away from that guy. He's an alcoholic. Don't talk to him," but there was something about his face that was so inviting, genuine and calming. He wasn't devastatingly handsome or tremendously well-built. He was just a medium-height, average-weight, lean guy, like a runner. He had a certain unmistakable, quiet confidence that I found very attractive. And once he answered my question about dying, I desperately wanted to talk with him some more.

We kept chatting for the rest of the bumpy, three-hour plane trip. He obviously noticed my distress and comforted me along the way with casual conversation. He asked about my career, and I asked him about his. Then he asked me what kind of music I liked. I explained I was a composer/teacher and had a passion for Christian Rock. He seemed struck by this response (like a woman who wears leather and red high-heeled boots couldn't possibly be a Christian). We bantered back and forth, and it kept me distracted; he kept me from thinking about imminent death, for sure.

When the plane landed, I was shocked that it was over so quickly. It felt as if, "Wow, time flies," (literally and figuratively)!

At some point, the nondescript, vanilla gentleman in the aisle seat became mesmerizing to me. I was intrigued by him and continued to engage in conversation. Steve was so endearing and really listened, looked me in the eye and didn't look away or glance at his phone or do stuff that a lot of guys do. He focused on me, and that was appealing as hell.

When the plane landed, I was relieved that we were on the ground, safe and sound, even though I had to get on another plane to go to Albuquerque. Thank God, the flight from Denver to Albuquerque was short and sweet.

We finally landed, and he walked with me and helped me with my bags. He said, "Would you like me to walk you to your gate?" I said, "Yeah, that'd be awesome." He walked me to my gate, and we exchanged business cards. He said, "Here's my card." I reached into the deep, dark abyss of my handbag and pulled out my business card and handed it to him, "Oh, here's mine."

I had told him that I wrote music and have songs on my website that he could listen to that were professionally recorded. He had said, "I would love to listen to your music." My website was on my business card. We talked about that. Then I asked him, "What exactly do you do for a living?" His reply was, "I make too much money." My heart immediately sank, "Oh, man, did he just say that? What a pompous ass he is." Then he laughed it off and said, "It's just because of taxes," or something like that. I replied, "Oh, okay. I don't have that problem." He laughed quietly to himself and said, "I will definitely listen to your music, and it was a pleasure meeting you." I thought when we parted ways that I would never see him again.

After we parted ways, I started thinking about some of the things he had said. The beer and the Merlot thing struck me as weird. Steve explained he was trying to figure out a way to sober up. He thought maybe drinking "the hair of the dog" would help. Who gets sober by drinking more? I thought that was interesting. Then, when he made the comment, "I make too much money,"

I took that as pompous and arrogant—him trying to say he's a money man and I should be with him because he has too much money. After that, he said, "Oh, it's the taxes thing. I pay so much in taxes. I wish sometimes I didn't make quite as much money." I reiterated, "Well, I don't have that problem so I wouldn't know."

But I could not get Steve off my mind. A day or two later, I sent him an email and said, "Hey, it was great meeting you. Did you listen to my music? What do you think?" And I said boldly, "If you're not involved with someone seriously and you're not married, if you're not in either of those two situations, we should get together. You're only a six-hour drive or a 45-minute plane ride away." I was satisfied with my email, so I sent it off. He responded pretty quickly and said, "Great, what are you doing this weekend?" I was flabbergasted because it was so quick. I thought, "Oh, that's like this Saturday, three days from now." Then I thought, "Jeez, why not?" He'll stay in a hotel. I stressed the hotel rather than my house. He said, "Great." I gave him directions, told him where I lived, and we made plans to meet.

As another day went by, I thought, "This is crazy. What if he's a serial killer? I can't do it." I emailed him and said, "I have an appointment, and I'm was busy with work. I can't see you. I'm changing my mind." His return email is what swayed me to agree to see him, and created a spark. Maybe this was something more than I thought, with this man. He said I was a magnet. That was the line.

12

He boldly stated, "You were a magnet, and I couldn't take my eyes off you." I thought, "Wow, that's so cool. I've got to see this guy. I don't care if he is a serial killer." That was it. We set the date and time for our first meeting!

It was here. The date night with Steve had finally arrived! What should I wear? This question plagues me frequently. I decided on my favorite pair of worn jeans and a tight, knit, turquoise tank top. The weather was hot and steamy, and this outfit was comfortable and flattering. We met at the bar of the Marriott Hotel where he was staying. We had drinks first and then dinner in their fancy restaurant. There was a huge white piano there, and he said, "Play." I said, "Really?" But I had had some wine, so I was less inhibited, and I started playing my songs. He loved all of them. He's said, "That's so cool." He asked, "Do you know any Elton John or Queen or ...." I said, "I can't play the way Freddie Mercury plays, but close." I played some songs that I recalled from my sheet music. I believe it was Bohemian Rhapsody....

It's very complicated. It's an intricate piece, but I played a little bit of it, and he was so impressed. We had a wonderful night of intense conversation. I think I told him everything about my life, (which happens when I start drinking). I wanted to hear Steve's response to a particular question. "What's the craziest thing you've ever done?" He said, "One night I was in graduate school, and these girls asked me to come over to their dorm." I said, "And..." He said, "That's it." I said, "What?" "That's it?" I thought, "Oh, man, we can never be together because I've done so many crazy things and have had such a colorful past that I'm looking like May West, and he's John Wayne's twin!

He told me he had recently broken up with a girlfriend of five years, and had been divorced for 16 years. Since meeting me, he was convinced he made the right decision to end things with his girlfriend. He knew she wanted to get married, but he did not. Their relationship was convenient, with zero passion.

A few weeks later, Steve informed me he had moved out and rented a condominium of his own.

Steve said he was 45, soon to be 46. I told him I had no children. I had only been married once, and it was an awful marriage that ended because of abuse (physical and mental). No love lost there. I was young and stupid when I got married. He told me he had a beautiful daughter named Samantha who was 17. She was an avid soccer player and voted MVP on her team. He attended every one of her soccer games. He also stated they were very close. He mentioned he had a stepson, Timothy, whom he'd raised from the time he was two years old. I thought, "Wow, that's impressive."

I asked Steve if he wanted to have more children. I was 40, and my biological clock was ticking. He replied firmly, "Well, of course, I would love to have another child." I smiled brightly and said, "That was a good answer!" It was a relief he and I agreed about kids.

Turbulence

Steve and I were both believers. If the God thing didn't line up, it wouldn't have worked. Believing in Jesus and loving God were very important to me, especially if both parties want children. He explained that listening to my music (because I wrote Christian songs) helped deepen his faith; it awakened his love of God, and created a fire in him to get closer to the Lord. He had listened to some of my songs on my website before coming to Albuquerque.

Steve was very intelligent and soft spoken. He was reserved, which I thought was interesting because I'm the complete opposite. I'm loud and animated, and he was calm and contemplative. I kept thinking, "Well, opposites attract. That's what they say." He was meek, and he struck me as very wise. I had no idea what he did for a living. He tried to explain it, but I finally said, "Let's just leave it at you have a master's degree in geography, you created your own company called Latitude, and you make maps for the government."

I had continued to nod at the bartender every time my glass of wine got low. At this juncture in the evening, I was intoxicated. We were at the bar until we moved to the piano. Then we had dinner in the restaurant, and I'd already had four glasses of wine. It seemed as though the wine, the ambiance and the company were making me feel warm and giddy. I remember feeling like I was walking on air. Steve made me feel like a queen. Steve was so chivalrous and respectful. I never heard him utter one curse word the entire evening!

ALMOST SHATTERED

He asked me, "Do you want to come up to my room?" And I said, "Sure, okay." I giggled, "I certainly can't drive home." I drove my own car with the anticipation of leaving. I had no intentions of staying. However, several glasses of wine dictated the course of my evening.

We went up to his room, and he opened a bottle of a very expensive white wine, something French. He described it as earthy with a hint of tobacco. Steve was a wine buff, which was impressive because I had just started developing a real interest in different wines. He was telling me about it, and I'm drinking it, saying, "Oh, it's great, what a lovely bouquet (the only word I knew of when speaking about wine)." Then, he sat next to me on the bed, we started kissing, and he shut the lights; we fell together. I told Steve, "I'm a Christian woman and I feel convicted about being together sexually before marriage." He understood completely (which was a huge relief), and we held each other all night. I stayed at the hotel with him that evening, and I remember feeling extremely safe.

The next morning, we woke up and had coffee in the room, and I said, "I feel like a hypocrite because I told you I am a Christian woman with strong faith, and I just stayed here with you." Steve replied, "It's okay." I said, "Really? Because I feel a bit embarrassed." He said, "No, it's okay. I want to see you again. I want to see you all the time." I blushed, looked at the floor and mumbled, "Cool."

Our night together was dreamy from beginning to

end. He felt bad because he was part of the reason I stayed. He was cajoling, wanting me to stay. However, Steve respected my boundaries because that's the kind of man he was.

This was out of character for me. Usually, I would date someone and wait six or seven months before spending the night together. It wasn't my nature to get so close with someone on the first date. That's why I thought, "What is going on here? What is it about this guy that I just let go; I just let it happen."

It was not in my character to jump into a relationship so quickly. Steve never jumped in quickly, either! I was confused but excited.

Steve caught me off guard. I felt off balance, and had this incredible feeling churning inside me constantly. A mix of anticipation and butterflies. I thought, "This guy could be the one. He could be the one I'm supposed to be with forever."

As time went on, we began to establish some routines. We had our favorite restaurant, favorite song and favorite wine. He would come to Albuquerque every other weekend, and I would fly to Denver on the off weekends. Steve paid for all my flights and expenses. We decided early in the relationship that we would be monogamous.

During our courtship, we would frequent the same spot. It was a restaurant called Scalo, and we'd order Carpaccio and wine and talk endlessly. When I was in Denver, Steve showed me all the interesting sights like

ALMOST SHATTERED

Red Rocks, downtown Denver, and the mountains. We enjoyed each other's company. It was easy.

I was an avid exercise person. I didn't much like running, but I loved Cross Fit. I was crazy for aerobics, weight lifting and high intensity interval training. He was a runner since he was in grade school. Steve would run almost seven miles a day every day like it was nothing. I asked him, "Teach me how to run because I want to be like one of those women that love to run." I was hoping I would catch the fever. I never really did, but my running got a lot better. We would exercise together every day and have our favorite wine and tell each other stories about our lives.

As our intimacy grew on many levels, my love for Steve got stronger. We couldn't keep our hands off each other in the beginning. I couldn't believe that I was so physically attracted to someone who wasn't my type. If you looked at a snapshot of my other boyfriends, they were much taller and well built, but Steve was perfect. My adventure had begun, and it would be one hell of a ride!

During this time, I met some of his employees. They were just regular guys, techies, geeks, into computers and trouble shooting. Knowing how to work with computers was Steve's expertise. He loved Macs. He talked about the weather. He'd say something like, "Well, there's a Chinook coming in." I'd ask, "What's a Chinook? Did you just make that word up?" It turns out that it's an actual thing, when the wind is going one way, and something happens. I soon realized Steve was a fountain of knowledge.

It was the same with trees. He knew every name of every tree. That's a maple, that's a spruce. I couldn't tell the difference. At times, I felt inadequate, like I needed to start learning geography and maps just to have an intelligent conversation with him.

It was the same way with weather effects. He owned satellites in the sky. The satellites created their own maps. Then, for instance, when Katrina happened, he worked with Washington, DC and the coast guard to tell them how to get in and how to get out safely because all the street signs were under water. The Coast Guard and Red Cross had no idea of their location, but Steve could tell them their exact coordinates from a satellite map.

Our courtship was something of a fairy tale. One night he said, "I want to take care of you." That's what he said. I was spellbound and replied, "You don't have to take care of me, but you can care for me. I can take care of myself. If you want to care for me, I want to care for you." He said, "Okay. So, do you want to get married?" I said, "Okay." I said yes. I couldn't even believe I said yes because it was kind of scary, but I said it.

Then he asked me, "What kind of jewelry do you like? If I were to get you a ring, would you like ... smaller but better quality?" I said, "No, bigger with some imperfections is my preference."

He bought exactly what I asked for, a beautiful solitaire. It was at least two carats and simply breathtaking. I've always said, "Bigger is better."

The ring was lovely. Every time I looked at it, I felt happy. I felt this surge of joy rush through me. "Wow, I'm engaged to someone who's awesome, and life's going to be great." That's really what I thought, like a fairy tale, just like a fairy tale.

When he gave me the ring, we were sitting on the sofa in the living room of my house in Albuquerque. We usually did that with wine. We would talk and say, "Do you want to watch a movie or go to dinner? What do you want to do?"

This particular evening in July (only three short months since our meeting on the plane), he was acting nervous and fiddling around with his hand in his pocket. I had to ask him, "What are you doing, because you're acting weird?" He answered, "Nothing, nothing. I'm good." He cleared his throat.

I said, "Hey, if you have what I think it is in your pocket, please let me see it. We're adults. This certainly isn't our first rodeo."

I think he was going to get on his knee and say, "Kate, will you ...?" I said, "You don't have to do that. Just.... Just come on, I want to see it."

He gave me the ring. I was crying, and he was hugging me; I was so happy. I said, "It's beautiful. I love it. It's awesome." He said, "Look, it's real." He showed me the certificate of authenticity. I answered tearily, "I didn't doubt that for a second Steve." Steve recommended we get the ring insured right away. He told me who to call and what to do to expedite the insurance. Then, we had a beautiful night together. We stayed home and laid on my big, fluffy couch and imagined our future together as husband and wife. We also discussed logistics. Should I be the one to move? We looked at the reality of our situation. Steve earned four times more money than I did. He had a home in Colorado and a flourishing company. We both knew—especially if we wanted a child right away— that I would be the one to move.

He said, "I want you to meet my family." I was excited as heck and nervous. They lived in Kansas, and he always talked about his mom, Doris. His father had passed away years prior. He had one brother living. He lost another brother in 1994 to an epileptic seizure. We had both lost a brother that same year (mine died in an automobile accident), and he understood the agony of deep loss. That was something else we had in common.

I was so excited to meet his brother and mother. I would also be meeting his entire family, all sixty of them at the annual "Williams" family reunion. I asked, "Do you really think the reunion is the best time for me to meet everyone? Shouldn't we just meet your mom first?" He said, "No, it'll be great. They'll love you." I answered, "If you think it's a good idea, I'm in."

So, we traveled to Kansas for the big family gathering!

ALMOST SHATTERED

It was one week before our wedding. It was a complete nightmare. It was worse than I could have ever imagined.

It's a six- or seven-hour drive from where I lived to Kansas, and we took Samantha with us. Samantha had spent a long weekend with me in Albuquerque, so the three of us decided to ride together. The drive was hot, extremely hot, because it was July and it was Kansas, humid and sticky. I wore something very conservative, but yes, I had tattoos. I've had tattoos for a long time. My tattoos were showing, and I couldn't hide them in 103* degrees. I wasn't going sweat to death to cover up my ink.

My tattoos were visible on my arms and upper back. I wore a halter top that was high in the back and not low cut in the front. My shorts fell just above my knee, Bermuda shorts; nice outfit, I thought, for a reunion-picnic thing.

We arrived at Steve's brother's house sometime in the early afternoon. Their home was huge because Steve's brother is a multi-millionaire. He deals in hedge funds or whatever. I called them hedge hogs at the time. I had absolutely no idea what a hedge fund was, and frankly, I didn't care. The fact that Jonathan had money was not impressive to me. My grandparents were millionaires, and I was raised in wealthy suburbia. I had traveled all over the world with my mother and siblings by the time I was 22. Jonathan's money meant nothing to me; I was excited to meet the man, not his wallet!

We finally arrived after a long, hot drive. Steve parked

the car in their driveway, and we began our walk up the path to the main house.

We walked into the house, and the first words his mother said to me were, "Oh, can you hold this?" She didn't even look me in the eye. She handed me a plate of something, some type of appetizer. I said, "Uhhh, sure." I looked at Steve nervously. He said, "Oh, don't worry about it. Just walk it down to the pool." I said, "Okay, where might that be exactly?" There was no, "Hi, this is Kate. This is the woman I've been seeing, and we're engaged and we're going to get married in two weeks." None of that, or none of, "Hey, could I see your ring? I've heard so much about you." Nothing. It was, "Can you hold this?" I was shocked.... I thought, "Okay, it's going to get better. It has to get better. They probably feel a bit awkward, meeting me for the first time. Maybe Steve hasn't been in love with anyone in a very long time?"

Next, I met Steve's sister-in-law, who was hosting the reunion. She was a petite brunette with a gorgeous smile. She approached me and said, "Hi, I'm Marion." She just stuck her hand out in the way that you (I guess) should when you meet someone for the first time, and said, "Hi, I'm Marion," and walked away. That was it. I was surrounded by all these people who weren't looking at me or talking to me; I was invisible.

I tried to understand: The mother basically treats me like the help and says, "Here, hold this." Then the sister-in-law says, "Hi," and walks away.

ALMOST SHATTERED

Meanwhile, Steve was off talking to his brother, getting a mixed drink because his brother is an expert mixologist. He had over 120 wines in his collection. He would always make some fabulous cocktail like a Caipirinha or something that tasted like it belonged on the menu of The Four Seasons. My fiancé was enjoying the company of his big brother. I thought, "That is so wonderful to have such a close relationship." Initially, I thought I'd be fine, thinking his family would embrace me; we would break the ice, and everyone could finally exhale. Steve's daughter, Samantha, with whom I thought I was developing a good rapport, left me to go visit with her cousins. I was standing there in the middle of a room filled with people, and was as lonely as I'd felt in years. I simply stood there, no food, no drink in hand… just standing there feeling like a lost puppy.

I remember I went into the garage where Johnathan had his seven cars, and I started crying. I was balling my eyes out, and I called my mom. I said, "Mom, this is awful. Maybe he's not the one. Maybe… his family hates me. They're awful. They're rude. They don't look at me in the eye. They don't talk to me. They don't want to talk to me. They didn't say congratulations or ask me any of the typical questions you ask someone whom you have just met…." I said, "I feel invisible." My mom gave me some sound advice and said, "You remember where you're from. You remember that you are a beautiful, talented, amazing young woman…." She gave me the whole mom talk. I began to take deep breaths and focus on what my mother had just said. I repeated to myself over and over, "You got this, Katie. You are smart. You are kind. You are worthy."

Then I went inside the house because there was a piano there. Marion had a daughter named Tory. Tory was learning to play the piano, so I sat next to her and said, "You want to learn some stuff?" She replied, "Yeah, cool." I was teaching her chords, the Circle of Fifths and all kinds of cool stuff. Then Marion came inside and saw us together. She abruptly shouted, "Tory, come here right now and take your meds. Take your medicine! You need to be outside." She didn't acknowledge me; she didn't say, "Oh, hey, Kate. How are you doing?" She just wanted her daughter as far away from me as possible.

I thought, "What is with this woman? What is wrong with her?" There was something so abrasive and something so incredibly cold about her presence. Tory, of course, listened to her and went scurrying away like a frightened mouse. I just stayed up there and continued to play the piano.

I struggled to understand what was happening and why. Could it be that Marion was feeling threatened and insecure? After all, as Steve's brother's wife, she was the star girl for all these years, the only daughter-in-law, the only woman in the mix. Suddenly, in walks Kate; tall, thin, attractive and smart. Not to mention my Italian culture where we hug, kiss and express every emotion under the sun! Maybe Marion felt threatened by my presence? Maybe she was afraid I'd steal her lime light?

I approached Steve a couple of hours later and said, "I need to leave. I'm leaving. You have to take me to the hotel. You can come back, but this is insanity. Your family's crazy. They're nuts. They don't want you to be with anyone. They don't want you to be happy obviously, so take me back to the hotel."

Steve said, "Kate, what's wrong?" I replied tearfully, "Your family's really weird. They're not like my family. My family's Italian. We embrace each other. We say, "How you doing?" We talk to each other. You want some food? We're very warm and "simpatico." We're that kind of people; that's what I'm used to, and we're touchy feely. We kiss and hug and touch and love! We're always touching." I continued, "Your family is so strange and cold. They don't even look at me; it's like I have the plague or something!! Steve, I felt invisible. It's uncomfortable, and I don't know what on earth I did to deserve this cruel treatment."

Steve said, "You did nothing. You did absolutely nothing! It's not your fault. I'll talk to Marion. Don't worry about it." I replied nervously, "No, don't cause a scene, for God's sake. Just take me back to the hotel."

I tried to understand the situation. The kids loved me, all the nieces and nephews, Marion's daughter, her youngest son, Trent, even her oldest boy Joseph, who was always in trouble, apparently liked me! The kids and teens at the reunion thought I was awesome!

I noticed some of the aunts and uncles acted strangely. Nobody really wanted to know me or wanted to know about our engagement or when we were getting married. Nobody showed any interest in Steve and me.

After the reunion, when we were driving back to Albuquerque, I said, "Your family is awful. I don't like them. They obviously don't like me." I said, "Actually, I don't know that I don't like them. They just don't seem to like me, at all. Nobody talked to me." I explained, "Steve, I have never been treated that way in my life. This is crazy." I said, "This is just so bizarre. You need to tell me what's going on."

He tried to explain that it was because he and Leslie (his previous girlfriend) lived together for years and were never married. He had been divorced from his first wife for eight years, but had a girlfriend for four or five years and had lived in sin, so to speak, and Marion was very Christian. She believed living together was a major no-no! You never live together. Living together was the ultimate sin! You must be married. She looked at Steve as if he was sinning. He said, "I think she assumes that we're sinning, (as he winked at me)."

I said, "You've got to be kidding me." I thought this was so ridiculous because a true Christian person would be warm and welcoming, regardless. Anyway, I said, "Look, if you still want to marry me, if you still want to do this, we're not doing it with any family." I continued, "We're getting on a plane. We'll go to Vegas and get it done." Steve replied, "That sounds wonderful." So, that's what we decided. Our wedding was actually planned during the drive away from that disastrous reunion!

Little Chapel of the Flowers is where we said our vows. The "package deal" was all inclusive, consisting of the hotel, limo ride, champagne, photographer and chaplain.

We decided to have a reception in September, two months later. During those months, I decided that I would leave my job and move to Denver to live with Steve and start our family. Steve actually was thinking about living in Albuquerque with me. He loved my little house and how easy it was to be there together. I said, "You know what? No! You need to be near your work. You make more money than I do. I'll find a job teaching piano somewhere. I can do my job anywhere. If we really want kids, I need to move and live with you in Colorado. So, we planned for me to move!

CHAPTER 2

Cracks

We did not say our individual vows at our wedding in Vegas. A Chaplain said the traditional wedding verse— "Do you take this woman?" We stood there, nervous as heck and repeated whatever he told us to say. It was a simple ceremony with Steve, myself, the Pastor and a photographer who doubled as a witness. The entire ceremony took only forty-five minutes. Feelings of anxiety and excitement stirred inside of me. The temperature was 103° outside, and that didn't help my intense nausea and looming headache from nerves. When the photographer asked us if we wanted any "outside pictures," Steve and I both shook our heads, "No, thank you!" The ceremony was over quickly, thank God, otherwise I may have fainted from the butterflies in my stomach. After the ceremony, I assumed the limo would drive us back to our hotel. Well, this was not the case. Apparently, after you pay the money for pictures, flowers, champagne and the limo ride from your hotel to the Chapel, they are done with you! You are on your own for transportation back to your hotel. I thought how could this be happening? It was so bloody hot outside, I felt faint. Steve and I decided to make the trek back to the WYNN on foot. We held hands and braced for the scorching sun and trudged our way back to our very beautiful, very air-conditioned five-star hotel. Once at the hotel, we collapsed on the bed and took a well-deserved nap!

After we were married, we flew back to Albuquerque. Steve stayed with me a lot although he was still living in Denver at the time. We continued in our normal, daily routines. I went to work, came home and called Steve. We would talk for hours. I loved his voice. He would leave after the weekend was over and go back to his work. During this time, part of our courtship was to eat at a restaurant called Scalo. It was a top-notch, ritzy Italian restaurant. We would have carpaccio and fresh-from-the-oven Italian sourdough bread, and wine of course! Steve was really into wine, and they always had great reds and whites in stock. Life was simple for us; a highlight we both enjoyed was our ritual of heading over to "our restaurant" each weekend. We were frequently seen sitting at the bar, laughing and talking. Our courtship was short but lovely, consisting of cool dates, romantic dinners and lots of fun.

We decided that we would have our reception in the month of September, so people could have time to plan and make arrangements to attend. We spent the entire month of August and the beginning of September planning the reception. We both wanted it to be perfect.

Cracks

The party was held at the Sheraton Hotel in Albuquerque, New Mexico. The banquet room was huge with small, elegant tables covered in black linen tablecloths. Every table had a small candle and our "mint–to-be" party favors. The party favors consisted of 2 silver bands (made of plastic) with white mints inside a tiny white mesh sack tied with a white satin ribbon. Each little sack contained a 2x2 card with a picture of Steve and me smiling. We hired a professional bartender and disc jockey for the festivities. The seasoned DJ had a long list of all of mine and Steve's favorite songs.

We decided not to invite Steve's evil sister-in-law, Marion. She and Johnathan, her husband, were against Steve getting married so soon after his break up with Leslie. They thought we should wait one year before getting married. Marion had only spoken five words to me since I'd met her, and Jonathan never spoke to me at all! Steve and I both decided not to invite them since they would be a sour note. We did invite his mom, daughter, and my family including my mom, sisters, and some of my closer friends. There were about 50 people, total.

At the big shindig in September, we said our own, personal vows. We wrote them ourselves and repeated them to each other in front of all those we loved dearly. I said something like, "I've never met a man who was so caring, generous and responsible." He really was all those things. He talked about how giving I was, that he never met a woman so compassionate toward others. He said

I loved to help people. He also said he adored my music. He ended with saying he was head over heels and would love me forever. The vows were not long and verbose, but heartfelt and succinct. We were truly in love and deliriously happy.

We danced to the Village People. We both were obsessed with music from the 70s and 80s. We have pictures of people with hardhats and cowboy hats doing the YMCA dance. We played a lot of Elvis, too. Our first dance was "Fools Rush In" by Elvis Presley. We both felt that particular song summed up the way we felt about each other.

There was a little drama during the evening. My mother's husband accidentally caught the tablecloth on fire. He knocked over one of the candles, and suddenly there was smoke and flames dancing on the table! Thank goodness, it was easy to extinguish. Then, my sister got sloppy drunk and started doing that whistle thing—you know, how some people can whistle really loudly with their two fingers in their mouths? She was whistling all around and hitting on my partner, Derek. He was my piano teaching partner. I had so many students, I needed to hire someone. Derek was a model, an incredible composer, and an extremely handsome young man. My sister started saying that she could suck golf balls through a garden hose. That was lovely. When I heard that sentence, I said, "Carla, you've had enough. You need to stop." My mom asked, "How do we get her off the dance floor?"

Cracks

Other than my mom's husband being clumsy and almost setting the entire hotel on fire and my sister coming on to anyone with a penis, it was a relatively benign evening.

We discussed children when we met. We both agreed we wanted to try for a baby as soon as possible. It was a miracle. In my previous marriage, I could conceive, but I was never able to carry to full term. It was a major heartbreak for me. Now, it all seemed surreal, "Holy cow, this really was meant to be," because everything just fell into place. Having children was very important to me because I was already 40, and I wanted my own family desperately!

I knew right away. I'm very in tune with my body. There were certain crystal-clear signs like morning sickness. I knew at maybe a month or six weeks. We didn't tell anybody until I passed the first trimester. We kept our mouths shut. I looked a little heavier in September at our reception but nothing obvious. Besides, I didn't care what people thought about Steve and me. I was experiencing a happiness I had never felt in my entire life.

Both Steve and I were strong believers in Jesus Christ. We wanted a biblical name, a name that was good for a little boy and good for a grown man. We kept coming back to Jack. It's a strong name for a little kid, and a man. I read in a book of biblical names I referenced that Jack was synonymous with John. Steve and I were both big fans of John the Baptist, so Jack seemed like the perfect name.

ALMOST SHATTERED

I was the happiest I've ever been in my entire life. Life was magical. I had a loving man who worked hard to provide for his family, a beautiful home and a baby on the way. Steve's sole purpose in life was to make sure I was happy. If I said I wasn't happy about something, Steve would find a way to work it out so I was. It's pretty incredible when someone demonstrates such sheer devotion.

Giving birth to Jack was another of God's promises. No issues, no complications, just bip, bam, boom, baby in your arms. After Jack was born, I worked intensely on getting my figure back. I spent hours in the gym every day at 5:30am with a trainer. Within 6 months, I was sliding into my size four jeans. Hard work pays off, I thought.

By October of 2007, soon after the reception, I moved to Denver. I was already sort of living there. I still had my house in Albuquerque, but I moved my things and settled in Denver. I asked the owner of the house I was renting if he would keep my security deposit and let me out of my lease early. He was a very kind man and said it was no problem. Steve went to work as usual, and I got a job at the USA School of Music, teaching piano and voice. I worked part time and took care of Jack and Steve. I cared for my baby, ironed Steve's work shirts, did laundry, made interesting dinners and was erupting with overwhelming joy.

The music school provided the initial ten students for me. Then, through word of mouth, my students would tell their friends about their piano lessons. The kids loved me. I loved the kids. They would tell their friends how much they enjoyed their piano lessons and within a week or two, moms and little ones would walk into the school asking for Kate! I had 30 students in no time. I felt blessed.

Steve was super helpful. The formula, the bottles, the baby food—he had it down. I was so appreciative of his help because I was exhausted in the beginning. However, Jack was an easy baby. He slept through the night by the time he was five months old. I remember thinking how amazing it was to be able to sleep until 5am.

When it came to Steve's job, he was as predictable and dependable as a clock. He would leave at 8:00am and be home by 5:30pm sharp. If it was 5:35, something was wrong. He was never late. He was extremely punctual. He was the guy you could count on. "Steve the Man," that's what I called him. When I met his coworkers, I thought they were typical computer geeks. The kind of people you made friends with in college to help you pass a really tough computer science class. They knew a lot about geography also, because that was part of their job. If someone asked me what my husband did for a living, I kept my reply short and sweet. I'd say something like, "Oh, he's a cartographer with the government, or he's a satellite map guy with the government." I honestly had absolutely no idea what my husband did for a living.

Steve never discussed his work. He wanted to talk

about my day, the baby and anything else but his job. "Well, how was your day? What did Jack do today? Did he roll over? Did he suck his thumb? Did he hold his bottle by himself?" Or he might ask, "Where do you want to go to dinner Friday night?" or "Do you want to watch a show?" He basically put work aside when he came home.

Initially, we lived in a small ranch-style house that Steve had bought as an investment. The woman who had been renting it moved away. He said, "Look, we have this house. Let's live here, and then we'll look for a place." It was a quaint ranch in a beautiful neighborhood in Colorado. The one draw-back we encountered with the neighborhood was, it was an adult community for folks 55 and older. Steve and I weren't even 50 at the time. So, we rented a house in a kid-friendly, soccer mom neighborhood when the ranch sold. After a period, we decided we knew where we wanted to live permanently. So, we bought a huge Cathedral-ceilinged, fire-places-in-the-wall type of home in a wealthy neighborhood close to great schools for Jack.

I had the impression that Steve was very affluent. I believed there was nothing to worry about financially. He handed me five credit cards and said, "Here you go, have fun!" This made me uncomfortable for reasons I can't explain. Maybe it was too much freedom? Maybe I felt I couldn't trust myself around high fashion? Or maybe I just wanted some accountability? There was only one time that I overspent; I felt extremely guilty after leaving the store with bags overflowing with amazing clothes! The day I spent that money on clothes, I approached Steve that evening and said, "You know, I'm not comfortable. This isn't okay with me." I don't know what I felt. I just didn't feel right, like I wasn't being a good steward, or something.

I suggested, "Let's get out of credit card debt. Let's cut them up! We'll keep one, for medical stuff, or for airline tickets, but let's stop using the others. Let's do the Dave Ramsey thing and save money." Steve was on board with my big idea. We ordered the CDs and listened to them. We did everything that the man suggested to do. I was recording everything I spent. I used cash and no credit cards. I assumed Steve was doing the same thing. I was so proud of us! Unfortunately, I discovered some years later Steve wasn't on board with my idea at all. He simply said yes and made me believe he was following the plan.

Steve preferred to pay our bills online; he was the king of the passwords! I jokingly would refer to him as my "secret agent man!" Then I would dance around the room singing that old song, "secret agent man, secret agent man, etc." I trusted him completely with every cell in my body, I trusted. I never gave money, bills or finances a second thought. I knew Steve would take care of everything.

He explained to me one evening, "All you have to worry about is taking care of Jack. If you want to go to work, that's great. If you don't, that's okay, too. Whatever makes you happy, sweetheart." He went on to say, "As long as you're happy, I'm happy." I had absolutely no idea how to pay the electric bill, water bill or mortgage. I believed I had married a wealthy, responsible, successful man. However, I wanted to be an asset to my husband, not a detriment. I believed advocating for no credit card use was a big help.

At the time, it seemed that whatever I wanted, I could have. If I saw a diamond ring that was really beautiful, buying it was fine with Steve. A dress, perfume, whatever. Anything for Jack as well, like the cool "BOB" stroller that allows you to run and stroll at the same time. Whatever I desired, I could have. There was no limit. Steve never said, "No." We traveled constantly, dined out, bought expensive decor for our home, and there was never any hint of financial concern.

My social life was slowly beginning to bloom. I began to make friends at the School of Music, my gym and church. I cared for Jack without a nanny until he was 14 months old. At that point, I hired a young gal who was referred to me by Steve's secretary (whom I really liked). Steve's secretary's name was Linney. Linney told us she had a close girlfriend who adored children and needed some extra income. "My girlfriend, Elizabeth, has a sales job that she's not happy with. She has a college degree in art therapy (which I thought was great), and she needs to supplement her income because the company cut her hours from five days to four each week." It was perfect, I thought. Elizabeth could work for us one day a week, and I could go food shopping or get my nails done or just sit on the sofa and read a book if I wanted! I was so excited to meet Elizabeth and have her meet Jack.

Things seemed to be slowly getting better between Steve's family and me. When Steve first told me his family was from Manhattan, I assumed he was referring to New York. I said, "Oh, that's so cool, me too. I'm from the East coast." He chuckled, "No, not that Manhattan, the Little Apple, not the Big Apple." I replied, "I never knew there was a Little Apple!" It seemed I was getting much closer to Doris, Steve's mother. Over time, I had grown very fond of her. She reminded me of Mrs. Claus, (Santa Claus's wife). She had white hair, she was pleasantly plump with a rosy-cheeked smile, and her laugh was infectious! She was a simple country woman who adored gardening, wearing her floppy sunhat and working in the afternoon sunshine. She planted flowers and baked bread. For me, Doris encompassed the ideal version of what a "mom" should be. She resided on a farm in Kansas. We visited the farm once every four to five months. Doris worshiped Steve. One day when we were sitting in her beautiful sun room, she told me how grateful she was that I was instrumental in bringing her son back to the Lord. There were tears in her eyes as she explained how wonderful it felt knowing her boy was attending church, praying and involved in a Bible study. I was truly moved by her kind words. I smiled and gave her a big hug.

ALMOST SHATTERED

As time passed, I wondered why Steve and I were the only family members who traveled. I asked Steve this question one day, "Why doesn't your family ever come here? We have a big house. We have lots of room." His answer to my question was, "That's just the way they are." I didn't understand that. It was frustrating. I loved seeing my mother-in-law. Jack loved the farm. I thought to myself, "You know, we'll just do it, and it'll be okay. Maybe someday they will accept my invitation and make a trip here?"

In the big picture, life was good! We took a yearly vacation to California or Miami, attended church every Sunday and did yard work together on the weekends. The ultimate picture of a wholesome, Christian, all-American family. That's what I thought I finally achieved! I'm finally normal, I thought to myself. I never really felt normal until I was with Steve. Steve was easy. He encouraged any endeavor, dream or idea I would throw at him. He was a good man. He never expressed jealousy, insecurity or inappropriate anger. We brought out the best in each other. In the past, I remembered feeling like the "black sheep" or the "misfit." I wore many masks to please whomever I was with at the time. With Steve, I didn't wear a mask. I was not a chameleon. I was authentic. The fear of finally exhaling was no longer present!

I was very involved with the church we attended. If I wasn't teaching Sunday school, I was playing keyboards on the worship team. Steve and I preferred the nondenominational church, solid biblical teaching without being watered down. Music was my favorite part of worship. I felt joyful, praising God and lost in the wonder of His blessings. It's an incredible feeling. I was on fire for the Lord when I met Steve. Apparently, that fire was contagious, and Steve's faith grew exponentially during our relationship.

One Sunday during church, I started looking around at the other men, the other husbands and dads. Then I looked at Steve. Something just prompted me to look at him with fresh eyes… I don't know why. His posture was horrible. He was hunched over, really hunched over. His back was almost rounded; it started to curve, as in a c formation. I looked at the other men, and it struck me that even the older fellows in their 70s didn't have that curve. There's something going on. I knew it deep in my soul. Something was wrong.

I wanted to believe that the gym could fix it, or a chiropractor. When we were leaving church, I said to him, "Dear, you're going back to the gym. This is ridiculous. You have to work out. You've got to go see Dr. Jay (he was our chiropractor) because your posture's horrible. You look like you're 90 years old." This is how I'd talk to him. I would just speak freely and say, "I'm worried about you. I really want you to be proactive about your health!" He was all for it. He said, "Okay, I 'm just feeling tired. Maybe it's the work."

Then, after I noticed this physical change in his posture, which was extremely obvious when he was standing still, I also observed that he was shuffling his feet. He wouldn't pick them up off the floor. His speech was garbled. Steve was a very soft-spoken man to begin with. Sometimes when he spoke, I had absolutely no idea what he was saying. I would just nod my head and say, "Yup, me too, aha, aha..." With the disease manifesting, of course, we didn't know it at the time, but it made that symptom even worse. I thought he was drunk. I actually thought, for a moment, he had a drinking problem. I said, "Did you just go to a bar? What the hell is wrong with you?"

My friends noticed, especially my girlfriends who only came over once every six weeks or so. They said to me, "What is wrong with him? Is he okay? Is he sick? Is he high?" They knew something was awry.

His whole affect was changing. He looked like he aged two decades. In our wedding picture, he looked maybe 35. When I first noticed something glaringly wrong, he resembled an old man. I noticed he was getting that turkey neck, the kind of neck where you don't have a defined jaw. The change was so subtle at first, I didn't see the difference. However, when it finally hit me, it was like a sledge hammer full force! There was no denying that something was happening to my husband beyond his control.

Steve loved to run. He ran the first two years of our marriage. The third year we were married, around 2010, he started slowing down a little bit. We got a treadmill in the house. He would run on that rather than go outside.

He was exercising less, but he was still exercising. I even brought him to my gym. I had him lifting weights, stretching and doing some balance work. This seemed to help a little, but not enough to change his appearance.

Steve still got up at the same time every morning and went to bed at the same time every evening. He insisted on driving to work by himself daily. I was concerned because his reflexes were not as sharp as they used to be. I was afraid he would have a car accident.

In May of 2012, we did "The Rugged Maniac" together. It was one of those wild mud runs, not the twelve mile one. It was a six mile run, with twenty obstacles, in mud. This particular day in May, it was a frigid, forty degrees and raining. I was excited and nervous. Steve seemed as calm as a cucumber. I assumed it was because he ran almost every day of his life for the past thirty years! I noticed, however, that I was always ahead of him, which was crazy because I wasn't the runner, he was. I thought, "Maybe it's the mud. Maybe it's because his shoes are bigger and they're sticking." I didn't know.

I also noticed on the very high obstacles, that required climbing, he froze at the top. I stood there yelling, "What are you doing?" All these people were running by. It was extremely muddy and wet, and we were trying to finish the race. He said, "I'm dizzy." I'm thinking, "Oh, God, he's going to fall. This is great. It's going to be all my fault if

Steve gets injured." He finally made it over the obstacle. He told me days later, "I've never experienced anything like that before. I got really dizzy when I was up high." He moved slowly, but finished the race. After this mud run, I insisted Steve see a doctor. I practically yelled, "Hey, go see your primary care guy as soon as possible!"

Steve finally agreed to see his doctor. I requested, "Get some blood work. Make sure everything is okay." He came home, and I said, "What did the doctor say?" Steve replied calmly, "I have vertigo. That's what's going on." I sarcastically said, "You're kidding. Right? It's not just vertigo." I remember telling Steve, "There's no way it's just vertigo." He replied, "No, he took blood. I had to do all this stuff. He took my vitals. He asked me a bunch of questions." I asked, "Okay, so what do we do for that?"

So, at first we both thought he needed to go to the chiropractor for his posture and that he just needed to eat healthier. But he couldn't eat like he used to and not gain weight. The man weighed 145 pounds when I married him. He was thin and lean. His weight had started to climb. We both noticed his weight mostly because his size 32 pants did not fit anymore. I wanted to believe with all my heart that it was vertigo. This dark cloud kept looming over me. Deep in my soul, I knew it was much more than vertigo. I pretended for a while because it felt better to stay light and in sheer denial than live in the harsh reality of the unknown.

You could still understand him, sometimes. His voice

had softened even more than usual. He could still enunciate, but there was no volume to his voice, no power. Steve participated in that mud run for me. He knew it meant the world to me to start and finish the mud run together. I know it was hard for him, but he did it. We finished in less than two hours. It was an experience I would never forget. The freezing rain, the mud everywhere, people cheering, and my husband and I facing it together until the end.

From May to December, Steve's decline was incredible. He started to look so old. He gained a ton of weight. I kept buying him new pants. He went from a 32 waist all the way to a 34, a 36, incrementally, until it was up to a 40. I had to keep buying him new pants because his jeans didn't fit in the tummy. His stomach was distended from whatever was going on in his body.

I said, "You've got to go back to the doctor. Let's see if it's still just vertigo."

When he went back in 2012, the doctor said, "Maybe you have vertigo. That's a possibility. However, I'm seeing some other things." Steve's PSA level was a little off. His blood work was off, too. They referred him to a neurologist to have a complete work up. So, we went to two different doctors, a urologist and a neurologist.

The urologist in May discovered that Steve was retaining fluid in his bladder. He was walking around with 400cc's of fluid he was unable to expel. That's why he was so distended. Then, in May of 2012, he started to have to catheterize himself every day for the rest of his life.

For a while, we thought we found the solution with the catheter. Steve was more comfortable. He walked better. He wasn't as distended. I thought, "Maybe that's all it was. It was just a bladder thing."

In June, we went on vacation to California, to the Hotel Del Coronado, in San Diego. We always took a nanny with us when we travelled. Elizabeth was studying to be a photographer, so she would practice her skills on us. Elizabeth was one of the most strikingly beautiful young women I had ever seen. With her lustrous long hair and her crystal blue eyes, Elizabeth was a stunner. Her inner beauty matched her outer beauty, which made her even more attractive. We decided to have pictures on the beach. Steve could walk from the hotel onto the sand with ease. Elizabeth took many candid photos of me, Steve and little Jack frolicking on the beach. Once again, we portrayed the image of the "perfect family."

During our vacation in San Diego, something happened that I will never forget as long as I live. Steve decided to go for a run one afternoon. The sky was blue, the sun was bright, and the day was absolutely perfect for a run. I was happy he decided to get some exercise on vacation. I was at the pool with Jack and Elizabeth when I realized what time it was. It was 3 pm, and Steve was not back from his run. He had left at 12:30 pm. I decided to head up to the room to see if maybe he was resting. When I opened the door to our hotel room, I saw my husband in a fetal position on the floor holding his head. I ran to him and said, "Oh my God, are you ok? What's wrong? What hurts?" He moaned and said, "My head is killing me; I can't open my eyes it hurts so much." I grabbed some ice and some Advil and gave him both immediately. Steve did not return to his normal self for at least two days.

Being with my husband daily, I didn't see the deterioration as clearly. Looking back, his walking deteriorated, his speech deteriorated, and his weight gain was significant. Everything hit all at once. From June to December, it was like night and day. He still went to work, but he changed his hours. He began to work 12:00 noon to 4 pm instead of the usual 8:00 to 5:30. Mornings were incredibly challenging. I had to dress him, shave him, and help him eat his breakfast. He insisted on going to work every day.

He exercised as much as he could because he said he felt almost normal when he walked on the treadmill or rowed on the rower.

After doing a ton of research on nutrition and Parkinson's disease, I discovered the best food plan for Steve was a high-fat, moderate-protein, low-carb plan. Carbs and sugar were absolutely no good for Steve. Protein had to be moderate, so the absorption of his meds was sufficient. The high fat was supposed to help with energy, blood sugar and over all wellbeing. I cooked all his meals and made sure he had everything he needed.

In December of 2012, we went to see a neurologist. He was very young. I asked, "Really, you're the doctor?" We were sitting there in his office, and I'll never forget the doctor's examination of Steve. It's as clear as day to me. He made Steve lift his right hand, lift the left, turn right, turn left. I blurted out suddenly, "He has Parkinson's, doesn't he? It's Parkinson's."

My grandma had it at a late stage in life, and I worked with some people who had Parkinson's. I was a personal trainer at this point. I had renewed my certification and started training clients at my local gym....

I mentioned it to Steve one time. I said, "It looks like you have Parkinson's." He said, "No, don't be ridiculous. That's crazy." Other people had said that he had symptoms mimicking Parkinson's. He didn't have the tremor, but he had almost every other symptom.

I asked the neurologist, "Is it Parkinson's? Is it our worst nightmare?" He replied, "Yep. It's generic, run-of-the-mill Parkinson's." I started crying. Steve just stood there. I said, "Okay. What do we do? What's the protocol?" He said, "Well, I'm going to put your husband on specific medication that helps with the symptoms of PD. I begged the doctor to please explain to me what these medicines do for the brain and body. Steve was stunned. I was asking all the questions. He gave us the report and the prescriptions, and said, "See you in six months." I was shocked, "You're kidding. Are you serious? Six months? Don't you want to see him next week, or the week after?" The doctor looked at me strangely and said, "No, just have your husband take his medicine every day, and he'll feel better." Steve took the medication like clockwork. I made sure of it. There was no improvement, none whatsoever. He just kept getting worse.

Steve took the medication that the doctor recommended. I started researching Parkinson's like a crazy person. I found the Davis Phinney Foundation, which provided locations of support groups and all kinds of information about Parkinson's. It explained the three different types, which the neurologist neglected to mention. I kept thinking, "Michael J. Fox has Parkinson's, and he's still acting and looks great! Maybe everything will be ok?"

I was hoping for more support from the church at this time, but that did not happen. No one offered to cook a meal, sweep my floor or to just sit down and chat. This was a very dark time in my life. We were attending Calvary Chapel, and I had Jack in a Christian school, but neither the church nor the school gave us any help or support. They'd say, "Praying for you, sister" and walk away. "How phony can you be?" I pondered as the woman whose daughter I taught piano for two years and saw weekly just sprinted away from me after a very awkward, very fake hug and sentiment.

During that time, I was working at a gym called Body Work, a Cross Fit Gym. I had been working out there for a year or two. My boss, named Mike, said to me out of the blue one day, "You're great with kids. You've got to teach the kids. Get certified. Just do it." I said, "Really?" I had been a trainer in my 20s and 30s. I always did it part time. I thought, "All right, I'll get Cross Fit certified." This was a huge undertaking, but I did it in less than six months. I studied and passed the test the first time.

I started studying in late 2012. First, I completed the Cross Fit training. Then, the next month I completed the kid's certification. They're two separate certs. I also earned a certification in Nutrition. I just kept studying, getting more books, going to more courses, and getting lots of certifications. It kept me busy. It allowed me to help Steve more.

For instance, I learned about gait training and fall prevention. Now I knew to say, "Honey, let's work on your balance, or let's work on stability." For example, he would practice holding two tennis balls in his palms and trying to walk a straight line.

Steve was very cooperative. He trained at least three times per week. In reading about Parkinson's, I learned that cardiovascular, cycling, rowing, and walking can be life changing. The exercise stimulates the brain and helps produce dopamine (which is lacking in Parkinson's patients). Cardiovascular activity can even halt the symptoms, according to many studies.

We began the typical protocol for Parkinson's, but Steve was not improving. We tried everything. As things progressed, life just got so ridiculously hard. I remember feeling like I was in a prison. A real prison. That I would never be like other women. I would never grow old with my husband and go to France, or Italy or any place where couples go when they're older and retired. I would never be able to look forward to those things. Steve may not make it to see Jack graduate high school. He may not be around for Jack to graduate from kindergarten! It was truly horrible. I went through bouts of depression. I started to drink alcohol more. I had to have wine every day instead of once in a while. It was like, "Well, it's 4:00 pm, it's wine-thirty, somewhere." They say caregivers can start to abuse substances. I did that for a while; it seemed to ease the pain.

I remember that my life, instead of being hopeful and happy, became this dark place, where I felt as if I were suffocating. I couldn't breathe. Finding out Steve had Parkinson's was one thing. Then, the meds didn't work. Next, there were all the exercises we tried. I even had him do the Lee Silverman Voice Training, otherwise known as LSVT. I found everything that I thought would help. Nothing seemed to leave us with the result we were looking for. You know when you know? You just have a feeling. I knew something was terribly off with my husband.

I remember going to dinner on my birthday. We went to dinner at our favorite restaurant here in Denver. It's called Nonna's, a gourmet Italian restaurant that reminded us of our Albuquerque days. His handwriting wasn't legible anymore because Steve had a condition called microphobia, where you lose the ability to write legibly. At my birthday dinner, Steve wrote me this beautiful letter and read it to me. I was so touched. He typed it on the computer in a beautiful font and handed it to me at the restaurant. The note said I was the woman of his dreams and he couldn't imagine his life without me. I cried as I read the beautiful note. It was heartbreaking. That's when I realized once again, his undying love for me. I'm not leaving him, no matter how much I wanted to leave. Everything in me just wanted to run, take Jack and run. That was fear. Fear is the absence of love. I thought if I love, and stay with those pure emotions, I'll be fine.

Later that year, somewhere in the middle of 2013, Steve started having to sleep in the downstairs room and couldn't sleep in our bed anymore. Then, sex became a problem. That was when Steve decided he wanted to go see the doctor. He couldn't make things happen anymore. He said, "Hey, not only do I look like this. I can't even have sex." They gave him Viagra. That didn't work. Nothing seemed to help. For more than two years, we had no sex. I would shrug it off lightly and say, "Don't worry about it. It's okay. I love you. Love isn't just sex." I would tell Steve I loved him no matter what, "I love you. I love hugging you. I'll snuggle with you downstairs before I go up and put Jack to bed." I remember for more than two years we had no sexual relations. Kissing was even difficult.

Part of the reason I felt so imprisoned was the lack of

physical intimacy. There was no touching, no lingering glances, no kissing, no physical contact, whatsoever. The intimate, erotic dynamic between husband and wife was gone. Steve was not able to express it in any way. His facial muscles seemed frozen and stiff. I never realized how hard it would be living with someone who can't show emotion. It was devastating. If I wanted to share my feelings with Steve, if I was crying or angry, he could not comfort me. He would just sit there and look at me with a flat, robotic gaze and say nothing.

We decided to see a new neurologist named Dr. Monica Gerard. She was the number one movement specialist in the country. I asked her, "Do you think Steve may have ALS?" She looked at me and replied, "Let's do the testing and find out for sure." Dr. Gerard scheduled Steve to undergo the testing for ALS. We walked into a different floor of the same hospital one week later. The doctor was surprisingly attractive. She introduced herself, and her smile was intoxicating. She had an air about her that was simply captivating. Anyway, she asked Steve to lie down and relax. Relax? Is this woman serious? He is about to be prodded with an electric impulse wand all over his body! Steve was obliging, and the test began. It was very difficult to watch. Every time she put the wand on his body, he would jump as if being shocked. I remember watching the doctor's face, and thinking, "This doesn't look good." When the test was over, I said, "Well?" She looked at me and nodded her head in a "yes" manner. I asked, trembling, "Does he have ALS?" She said, "I believe he does." What happened next was mind blowing. The doctor left the room and never came back. I got on my knees in front of Steve, put my head in his lap and cried like a baby. We must have stayed that way for over 30 minutes. Finally, we both stood up, and we drove home.

I made a commitment to God, myself and Steve to be the best wife and caregiver humanly possible. I decided to embrace the idea of caring for Steve. I could be like Christopher Reeve's wife and simply accept this new situation bravely. I sure didn't feel brave, but I could fake it. The days fell into each other, and I became a robot moving through the motions of life.

I dressed Steve and shaved him. I helped him do everything. He had difficulty moving. As the months went on from 2012 to 2014, we bought all the equipment to make Steve's life easier. The automatic chair that went down the stairs, the breathing machine, special utensils for eating, a shower chair, a walker, anything that would allow Steve to maintain some semblance of independence. Life became a one-minute-at-a-time pace for me. I rarely experienced joy, laughter or happiness. I longed to be joyful again one day. The longing in me was palpable. I'm sure others could see the sadness and pain in my eyes. Jack was my only joy. His laughter was infectious and his smile breathtaking. My son was my reason for hope. I had to fight to keep Jack's life magical and innocent.

CHAPTER 3

One Night of Freedom

O NE OF THE THINGS I DID TO FEEL BETTER and renew my spirit (something I desperately needed), was to find a Christian women's retreat. The retreat was an hour away, and I had been there several years back with women from my church. It was a weekend conference called something like "Being Refreshed."

I called my girlfriend Jules because she was going through a difficult time and dealing with a possible divorce. Jules was one of those women who never needed to wear makeup. She stood about 5'7", with shoulder length, dirty blond hair and had a smile that melted hearts. She was also the strongest woman, physically, I had ever met. Jules competed in Strong Man competitions (and won). She had four children and did everything with them and for them. It was obvious why I considered this woman my dearest friend. I trusted her implicitly. We were both in a dark place. I had a dying spouse, and she had a dying marriage. Jules agreed to go with me, so we made plans to attend the retreat the weekend of April 4th. Obviously,

ALMOST SHATTERED

I had to prepare to be away. Although it was for only one night, I needed all my ducks in a row for Steve's care.

I kept thinking, one night of freedom, of being able to sleep and not having to listen for noises or worry if Steve was awake or still breathing. The thought of not having to do the morning routine of blood pressure, pulsox, changing sheets, dressing and shaving Steve was a relief. Just one day's reprieve, I thought, would be a dream. This was my plan.

I hired a CNA to come to the house and stay with Steve until he went to bed. She would administer his meds, check his ASV machine (breathing apparatus) and make sure he ate some dinner. Steve loved to eat! I made him three of his favorite dinners and said, "Hey, you've got three fabulous meals to choose from." I asked him ten times if he was really ok with me leaving for one night. He replied, "Of course, have fun, you need this."

Jack was staying with Liz, my dear friend and nanny at the time. He loved sleeping over at Liz's house. Elizabeth loved Jack as her own, and Jack adored Liz and her husband, Allen. Liz and Allen treated Jack like a prince! They took him out to eat, played hide and seek and did just about anything to make my little boy happy. I never worried or gave Jack's well-being a second thought when he was with Elizabeth.

Steve and Jack were covered, and I thought everything would go as smooth as silk. I would get to be away, experience a night of freedom and feel renewed by God's inspiring word.

We had to check in for the retreat by midnight. If we left around 6pm, we would miss the bulk of traffic and get there early enough to get settled in our room. Leaving around 6 pm allowed me to make sure Steve had his supper and meds, and I could introduce the CNA to him personally. Steve was delighted with his choice of dinners, and Jack was as happy as a clam hanging out with Liz and Allen. One night off wasn't a lot of time, but it was plenty for some heartfelt laughter, intimate girl talk, and a few select alcoholic beverages.

It was 6:30 pm on a Friday, April 4th when Jules and I hit the road. The women's retreat was only an hour away, and Steve had recommended a fabulous steak house called Duke's for us to try before arriving at the women's retreat. He said, "Make sure before you get to Castles of Old (which is where the retreat was), you go to Duke's Steak House." I asked, "Are you sure?" He smiled and said, "Of course, just go. Have a good time; have a few drinks and chill out." I thought, "Wow! That sounds amazing!" He gave us the directions, and we set off toward the restaurant, merely two miles from our destination.

I asked him over and over again, "Are you okay with me doing this? It's just one night, but if you don't want me to go, I won't." He replied quietly, "I don't like it when you and Jack are not here. I miss my family. (Steve couldn't watch Jack by himself; that was out of the question.) I said, "Hon, I need this. I desperately need this." He replied, "I know you do, and I want you to go and have a nice time." I comforted him by saying, "By the time you wake up and get dressed, I'll be home."

Something I remember vividly was Jules saying, "I don't think we should leave yet." I said, "What are you talking about? Everything is perfect. He has the dinners; the CNA is here." I was anxious to leave. She kept saying, "Let's just wait a little longer."

We got a later start than we initially wanted, but when Jules felt like the coast was clear, we left. We headed to Duke's. We had a wonderful evening. We ate steak that melted in your mouth like butter, and we had top-shelf California wine as we laughed our heads off about both our situations. Neither of us had had sex with our husbands in two years or more. Sex was something I believed I could live without. Although I dearly missed being with my husband, I knew God would give me the strength to carry on. Jules and I talked about our longings and how we wished things could be different. We laughed and talked, and both of us felt better.

It felt so comforting to confide in another woman who completely understood what I was experiencing. I told Jules this retreat was going to be a game changer. We were going to get renewed and not give up. We both agreed we would start over in our marriages with a clean slate (like an Etch a Sketch). Neither of us would ever quit on our spouses or ourselves, no matter what!

Jules had discovered her husband had been unfaithful. She was struggling with forgiveness and contemplating divorce. I did not judge Jules. I appreciated her and valued our friendship immensely.

After Duke's, we went to the retreat. The area was called the "Castles of Old," appropriately named because it was so beautiful. We checked in at the front desk area of the hotel, and they told us we were staying in the lodge. We weren't in the castle. There was a big old castle, and there were little lodges, like cabins on the campus. We drove my car to the entrance of our designated cabin and dragged our bags in awkwardly.

We finally got our suitcases into the room and closed the door. I was so excited to slip into my comfy pajamas and relax. I said to Jules, "This will be the first night in years I get to just fall asleep and not feel anxious. I can actually sleep!" I jumped on the bed like a little kid; Jules was jumping on the bed with me. We were laughing so hard, like kids. We were a little bit tipsy but felt so joyful. We had brought some wine with us and cracked it open. I was so excited, like a little child in a candy store! We poured the wine into our little plastic cups and made a toast to us. Suddenly, my phone rang. I looked at my cell phone, and it said, "Steve the man," (that's how I had his number in my phone).

I said, "Oh, it's Steve calling, let me get it. He probably wants to make sure we're okay." She said, "Sure." I answered the phone and said, "Hey, Hon." The voice on the other end of the phone said, "My name is doctor so and so, and I'm with your husband." I don't know if I can accurately describe the feeling that began in the pit of my stomach and trickled out to my entire being. I felt as though I was not in my own body anymore but watching this scene from somewhere else. I replied, "No, that's impossible." I was in complete denial. I said, "Why in the world do you have my husband's phone? What are you doing? Who are you? This is ridiculous. I just left him two hours ago, and everything was fine. This is impossible. Put my husband on the phone. Put him on the phone now."

He said to me, "Kate, that's you, right, Kate?" I said, "Yes." He said, "Your husband went out to dinner this evening." I said, "No. No, he didn't. Why would he go out to dinner?" I shrieked, "You don't understand. Look, I don't know who you are, or what you're trying to do, but if you don't put Steve on the phone now, I'm calling the police. This is wrong. You probably stole my husband's phone, right? It's stolen? You're some quack or on crack, or you're trying to get information from me?"

He replied quietly but firmly, "My name is Doctor Weinberg, and I am an ER doctor with Swiss Hospital." He said it again. "I work at Swiss Hospital in Englewood, Colorado. I am a cardiologist and a surgeon." I slowly began to realize the man on the other end of my cell phone was a doctor and was speaking the truth. I thought, "Oh, great. This is true. This is really happening. He is a doctor." I replied shakily, "Okay." I remember hearing my own heartbeat. My pulse and blood pressure were rising quickly, everything started to speed up. My adrenaline was pumping off the charts! All I heard was noise on the other end of the phone after he said the words, "Steve had a heart attack." He repeated, "Your husband has had a heart attack. They found him in his car in the parking lot of Chili's Restaurant."

I said, "Doctor, you don't understand. He was supposed to stay home. He wasn't supposed to go out. He wasn't supposed to go out without help. He said, "Kate, the paramedics worked on him for over an hour." I told the doctor Steve was a DNR. He wore a medical bracelet on his left wrist that stated this. I told him the bracelet had my number and Steve's doctor's number engraved on the inside.

He said, "The paramedics didn't look at the bracelet. Their job is to sustain life, no matter what. They probably thought it was a nice piece of jewelry. They worked on him, and brought him back. When they found him in the car, Steve still had a very faint pulse. The paramedics started doing CPR because they thought he had aspirated."

The doctor told me they worked on him for over an hour and brought him by ambulance to Swiss Hospital. He also said I needed to get there as soon as humanly possible. My voice was talking, but my brain had no idea what I was saying. I asked, "Well, is he okay? He's going to be okay, right? My husband has ALS. He doesn't have a heart condition. He doesn't have diabetes. He has ALS." The doctor said, "You need to get here." He said, "You really need to get here."

I spoke with some authority in my voice and said, "No, I have to know. Is he okay? Is my husband okay? He's going to live, right?" The doctor wouldn't answer my question. He was being evasive. I started screaming at the top of my lungs.

I think your body goes into shock when something you can't even imagine happens. It has happened, but you don't want it to happen, and so your body is protecting you. The first thing is denial. That's where I was. I started rocking back and forth like a lost child, rocking, holding myself, rocking and screaming, "No." I kept saying, "No, no," over and over, when Jules said, "Give me the phone."

I gave her the phone, and she was very calm and clear. She explained who she was, and she said, "You need to tell me what's going on. You just spoke to his wife, and she is not okay right now." The doctor said, "Look, I don't know what else to do; we need her here." Jules said, "We're on our way. Give us an hour. We'll be there." At this point, we got in the car. I remember how dark it was. It was pitch black, and we were in the mountains.

I was in shock, screaming my face off, repeating, "I want to see Jack. I want to see my son. I've got to get Jack."

Jules said, "Kate, you need to calm down. Just breathe with me. We're going to breathe together. That's all you need to do right now. Inhale, exhale, repeat. Just do that." I said, "Your right." Suddenly, I had a thought that maybe things were not so bad. Maybe the doctor was exaggerating. I looked her in the eyes and said, "Hey, it could be fine." I kept figuring out a scenario, like maybe he just had a heart attack and people recover from those all the time. I told Jules, "This isn't a big deal, we'll be fine. It's going to be good. We're good."

Then I would switch back to crisis mode, "Holy shit!! What am I going to do? This is... this can't... I can't live without him. I don't know what to do. How do I pay the bills?" Everything just came spewing out. I kept going back and forth from mitigating the situation to full blown crisis mode. Jules was as calm as a stagnant pond. She said, "You need to call people. You've got to notify some people, like his daughter, his mother, and his brother." I said, "Oh my God, you're right."

I asked her, "Do you think I should wait?" She said, "No, I think you should call right now." Luckily, I had all their numbers in my phone, and I started making frantic calls. I called his daughter, Samantha, and Samantha's husband, Martin. They were married at this point. There was no answer, so I left a message. I left a message for them on their voicemail saying, "Martin, Steve has had a heart attack; we don't know what his condition is, but he is at Swiss Hospital in Englewood. When you hear this message, go there immediately."

Then I called Marion, the evil witch monster, and Johnathan. Marion answered the phone and said, "Oh, hey Kate, what's going on? Is everything okay?" in her stupid, horrifyingly fake voice. I replied nervously, "No, nothing is okay." I don't know why I did this; I kept saying, "I only left for one night. I just left for one night." That's all I kept saying. Marion asked, "What are you talking about? What do you mean, you left for one night? Where are you?" I said, "I'm driving to the hospital."

I eventually got the facts out. I told her that Steve had had a heart attack and that I had planned one night away. One night in three years, and that's the night that it happened. She said, "What hospital?" I told her, and she said they would leave immediately. My next call was to Dick and Sue. Dick and Sue were our best friends, (or so I thought at the time). Sue was my dear friend, and Dick was Steve's best buddy.

We always hung out together. Dick worked for Steve. I called him, and I said, "Steve's had a heart attack. I don't mean to bother you guys." It was around 11:30 or midnight. It was late. They replied, sounding suddenly wide awake, "Where is he?" I said, "Swiss Hospital."

I found out later that Steve called Sue and Dick after I left for the retreat and said, "Hey, do you guys want to go to dinner?" They said, "We're busy." Their guilt was palpable. My guilt was eating me alive. We were all thinking, maybe this wouldn't have happened had we been with him.

After I made the calls, I remember thinking, "My life will never be the same. My life will never be the same again." I had a feeling that this was the end. I desperately didn't want it to be because I wasn't ready. I didn't feel prepared in any way, but I thought, "It's happening. This is it. It is happening." I called Liz because Jack was with her and said, "I want my son. You've got to bring me my son." She said, "Kate, he's asleep."

I said, "I don't care. I want my boy." I was out of my mind and in shock and felt like a wounded, cornered animal. She cried with me, and she said, "Do you really want me to wake him up?" I said, "No, no don't, but promise me, Liz." I continued, "Promise me that you'll bring him home to me tomorrow." She cried, "Of course, of course I will." The distinct feeling I had was that my world had just slipped through my hands and there was absolutely nothing I could do to change this. I actually imagined it was a conspiracy against me. That my husband and my son were being taken from me on purpose by some evil force. It was an irrational, paranoid thought that was perfectly normal, given the circumstances.

I actually believed Liz was going to keep Jack from me. Elizabeth, the most responsible, trustworthy person on the planet was conspiring to take Jack from me!! Man, I was paranoid! Oh, my God, I'm all by myself. What am I going to do? A million scary thoughts bounced around in my brain.

I was in shock. We were getting closer and closer to the hospital. When we finally arrived at the hospital, Jules parked in emergency parking, and I started running. I kept repeating, "I want to see my husband." We were running toward the entrance of the emergency room at top speed, (we're both athletes).

It was super late. The door slid open, and we walked to the reception desk. Winded from my sprint across the parking lot, I breathed, "Hi, my name's Kate Williams. I want to see my husband." The middle aged, extremely overweight nurse pushed her glasses up on her nose and in a snippy tone replied, "Well, you're just going to have to wait." I stood there, breathing back to normal, and just stared at her for what seemed to be an eternity. I finally repeated loudly, "I want to see my husband, now." She looked at me like, "Oh shit, this woman is nuts. Is she going to beat me up?" She said coldly, "Fine." Exasperated that I was bothering her, she walked me back to a little room divided off by a curtain.

She opened the curtain, and I will never forget the vision that filled my reality. As long as I am alive, I will never forget what my husband looked like in that moment. He didn't look like Steve. He was intubated, had IVs in both arms and there was dried blood on his chin and chest.

It was my worst nightmare. A machine was breathing

for him and there were tubes and lights and odd noises seeming to come from everywhere. He had blood dripping from the side of his mouth, and there was dried-up blood all over his shirt. I don't faint. I never have fainted in my life. Suddenly, standing in the hospital room, staring at Steve, the floor rushed toward my face. My son-in-law, Martin, caught me in his arms before I crashed to the ground.

I was expecting an entirely different scenario at the hospital. I thought I'd say, "How are you doing?" and Steve would say, "I'm sorry, sweetheart. Sorry I had a heart attack." Or "Sorry I went out to Chili's." That's not what I saw or what happened. He was extremely bloated and didn't look like himself. I hardly recognized him. I just looked at him, and I started to cry. Deep, guttural sobs erupted from my throat. I sat in the chair in the hospital room and wept.

I must have been a sight. Tired, scared, half dressed in pajamas, black mascara running down my cheeks and hair that hadn't seen a brush in over a day! Suddenly, I was aware of the nurses taking care of me. They were putting ammonia under my nose, taking my blood pressure and my pulse. They made sure I didn't need a bed next to Steve!

Instantly, it hit me! The date was exactly seven years from the day we met on that plane. Every time that date rolled around, we called it our second anniversary. The anniversary when we got married was July 21st, but we met on April 4th, 2007, flying to Denver. It had been Easter weekend, seven years prior. I thought, "Oh, my God, seven years ago today, I met Steve on the plane. This is more than ironic; it's crazy and kind of cool." I think I shared this with Jules, and then I shared it with Martin and Samantha.

Martin and Samantha said, "We're so sorry. Kate, we're so sorry." I wasn't angry with them. I was disappointed that they didn't come around as much as I had wanted, but I loved them deeply. I loved my stepdaughter dearly. Do I think she could have picked a better husband? Sure, but Martin was cool. He was a Godly man, and she loved him. They hugged me, and I kept saying, "What am I going to do? What am I going to do?" Martin replied gently, "We'll help you, whatever you need, whatever...." He continued, "Kate, it's going to be okay. We'll figure this out." I uttered through the sobs, "Okay." At that time, I was feeling positive about my relationship with them and thought maybe they would actually do what they said and help me through this.

Some hours later, the nurse and the doctor came over to me and asked, "Are you ready to talk?" I said, "Yes, I'm clear, I'm ready." I think someone brought me some water, and the doctor began telling me exactly what happened. They found Steve in his car, slumped over the steering wheel in the parking lot of Chili's. Someone made a call about a guy looking like he's asleep at the wheel. Paramedics came and worked on him for more than an hour... blah, blah. The doctor relayed the whole horrifying scene again.

I said, "Well, if he's had a heart attack, don't people recover from these all the time?" He said, "Yes, I had a guy last weekend who had a heart attack and two hours later was sitting up playing the guitar." I thought, "Oh, wonderful, that's good news." I felt reassured for a minute after the doctor spoke to me, and I said, "I guess he has to stay here for a little while." The doctor said, "Yeah, we need to do some more assessments. We're going to move him to ICU, and we're going to have another cardiologist look at him."

I gave him the name of Dr. Monica Gerard, Steve's neurologist, and all the other information he needed. It was between 2:00 and 2:30 am by that time, and the doctor looked at me and said, "You need to sleep. You've got to go get some sleep." I thought, "No, I can't, I can't sleep." He said, "Have you eaten?" I said, "Well actually, I ate earlier at a steak house my husband recommended." The thought of food was revolting.

I told the doctor what I was doing and why I wasn't with my husband that particular evening. He said, "Why don't you go home? I'll see you in the morning. If you want to come back at 7:00 am or 8:00 am, that would be fine."

Jules drove me home. Steve's family hadn't arrived yet because it takes about six or seven hours to drive from Kansas. I thought they would come to my house. I thought the natural thing would be to come to the house and we'd cook, cry, pray and help each other. I couldn't cook, drive, eat, or do anything a normal functioning human being does. I went home and went to sleep. I tried to sleep, anyway.

Jules stayed the night. I woke up in the morning, maybe three hours later. I took a hot shower and threw on some clothes. I noticed that when the hot water from the shower hit my skin, it felt like tiny razor blades on my flesh. I had become so incredibly sensitive to touch. If someone hugged me, it hurt. I remember thinking, this is what grief, death, loss and tragedy feels like. I had some coffee, and Jules and I drove to the hospital. Steve had appointed me power of attorney and medical power of attorney. I had the decision-making authority over everything, but I didn't bring those papers with me because I didn't think I would need them.

When we arrived at the hospital around 8:30 am, Steve had been moved to the ICU. There is a spacious waiting room on the ICU floor, and when I walked in, I immediately saw Marion, Johnathan, Doris, Samantha and Martin. They were all sitting next to each other with miserable looks on their faces.

Marion noticed me and half shouted, "He's critical. He's going to die. He's critical, Kate. Steve is not coming back from this." She looked me dead in the eye and said those words. It felt as though someone punched me in the stomach, and I couldn't breathe. Why on earth would she say these things to me? Why would she deliberately speak the worst scenario when I was hanging on to my sanity by a thread? I took a deep breath, composed myself and said to her, "No. No, that's not true. The doctors haven't said that to me. They haven't mentioned anything to me about critical condition or dying." I repeated, "He's had a heart attack, and that's all we know."

I felt a strange sense of empowerment and strength as I asked the evil witch monster to step out into the hallway with me. I walked toward her and got right in her beautiful but evil face. I looked her dead in the eyes and stated, "If you have something to say about my husband's condition, either keep it to yourself or speak with me privately. Don't ever do that again." At this point, I had no tolerance for her or her evil mouth. I didn't have to appease her for Steve's sake anymore. She never liked me—that was obvious—so why should I pretend to like her? The most ironic thing about Marion was that she practically screamed from roof tops that she was a devout Christian. This devout Christian woman could not manage to muster even a crumb of kindness, empathy or compassion toward me in this tragic situation.

It dawned on me that Steve's family must be staying somewhere, but they never came to my house. I asked, "Where are you guys staying? Where's your stuff? You're going to come to the house, right?" "No, we're not coming to your house," the witch monster replied in her snotty, haughty tone. "We're staying at a hotel right next to the hospital." I thought, "Wow, that's truly unbelievable." Nobody asked about Jack. My son was only five, just five years old. No one said, "How's Jack doing?" or "Where is Jack?" Not a word was uttered about my boy, Steve's only son, Jack.

Steve's family could have come to my house. I assumed they were coming to our house, but they chose to stay in a hotel by the hospital.

I remembered that Steve wanted Pastor Angelo to perform his Memorial Service. If something happened to him, Steve wanted Pastor Angelo and no one else. Pastor Angelo was the Pastor of the church we attended. It was known as Calvary Chapel. We had known Angelo for seven years or more. I thought I needed to make a call to him and let him know what was going on, especially with our need for prayer. When I called him, Pastor Angelo said he'd be there as soon as possible. I regarded Pastor Angelo as an ally. I was anxiously anticipating his arrival because what I desperately needed was an ally.

The doctors continued to work on Steve that day; he was hospitalized on a Friday and on Saturday, they continued with non-stop tests and assessments. They checked for brain activity. Every time they tried to bring him out of the coma or raise his body temperature, he would start to seize. He was seizing wildly, and I said, "Make it stop. Please, for the love of God, make it stop." On Friday night, they induced a coma and lowered his body temperature to help his body repair faster. They had these things on him that resembled tin foil. It was actually ice to help lower his body temperature. When the doctors tried to bring him back through the course of Saturday to see how he would respond, Steve seized again wildly.

He would throw his arms and legs about in a frenzy. First, I thought, "Is this good? He's coming out of it?" But the doctors were saying, "No, it's not good." The doctor said, "It probably means that his brain is not the same. That there's been some damage, extensive damage."

When the doctor spoke those words, "extensive damage," I remember thinking, "Steve didn't want to be a vegetable." He hated being poked and prodded. He hated doctors, in general. He didn't like going to them or following their advice. He told me on several occasions, "If something happens to me, I don't want to be resuscitated. Never risk me coming back as a cucumber."

At some point during all the activity, Marion started calling the shots (because she's a nurse and thinks she knows everything about medicine in general). I walked into the hospital, and I saw Marion conferencing with one of Steve's attending physicians. I grabbed one of the nurses and said, "She can't do that. What in the hell does she think she is doing? I have medical power of attorney! I am his wife!" The nurse replied, "Do you have that in writing?' I said, "I absolutely do." Jules drove me back to my house to get the papers, the will, and the documents.

ALMOST SHATTERED

I brought them back to the hospital, showed the doctor, and they kept the entire family out of his room, finally!

I thought, "Thank God." Steve's family wouldn't let me be alone with him. I wanted to lay next to my husband one last time. I couldn't because the evil witch monster, Marion, and her husband, Jonathan, would never leave the room. They wouldn't give me a minute just to be with him, just one last time. Finally, when they kicked the relatives out, I said, "May I lie with him?" The nurse looked at me with pity and sorrow in her eyes and said, "Kate, there's too many tubes." There were so many tubes and gadgets and beeping noises and lights, it was mind blowing. So, I stood over my dying husband and stroked his cheek with the back of my hand and cried.

The doctors continued to work on Steve intermittently. They observed him, analyzed readings, listened to his heart beat and watched for seizures. They brought in specialists—specialists on ALS and brain damage. A machine was breathing for him. He wasn't doing it on his own in any capacity. The doctor explained to me that if Steve was taken off the machine, he might live for an hour or two, and that would be stretching it. He said, "We're just waiting to see if we can raise his temperature again. Raise it to 98.6 or somewhere in that range, to see if he will respond positively." They did that three or four times. He didn't respond positively at all, which indicated brain damage.

They did another test for brain activity. The doctors

discovered that there was little to none. It was time to make a decision. In my husband's will, it states, "Five days if intubated" and "No coming back as a cucumber," (Steve's words). The reason he chose five days was to allow family to arrive. The family was already here, even though it had only been three days, so I thought Sunday would be the day to say goodbye.

Meanwhile, I wasn't eating. I wasn't sleeping. Late that Saturday night, Jules once again drove me home.

Sunday, I came back, and we all agreed that this was the day we would discontinue life support. It was on Sunday we uncovered that Steve had chosen to be an organ donor. This was really hard for me even though it was in the will. The doctor said, "His kidneys are good. We have someone who is in desperate need of a kidney. Someone waiting right now for a transplant. Kate, what do you say?"

First, I said, "No, you're not going to cut him up like a damn piece of meat. You're not going to touch him; he's my husband!" I kept saying that because the thought of someone just taking what they wanted from him made me sick. Finally, I said, "You know, that's what he wanted." I kept thinking, "It's just like Steve to go out a hero. Even in death, he is still helping people."

I agreed to the organ donation. After all, it was in Steve's will. It's what he wanted. I was honoring his wishes. That changed our plan because they had to keep him alive longer to do the surgery since organs can only last a certain length of time outside the body. Since it was already Sunday when we learned he was an organ donor and I finally agreed to the organ donation, we couldn't pull the plug and say goodbye because they needed to take him to surgery to do the transplant.

People from the Organ Donor Alliance approached me constantly to thank me for my brave and courageous decision. I said, "Look, just do what you've got to do. I need to take care of my little boy and somehow get through this." It was very difficult to look them in the eye, knowing what they were going to do to my husband. Although Steve was gone, I was still trying to protect him somehow.

Sunday was the day I said goodbye. Pastor Angelo had arrived and was present for myself and the family. He said, "Kate, you don't need to see what happens when they bring his body temperature back to normal. You certainly don't need to go to the surgery. Don't expose yourself to this; it will be traumatizing." I asked Pastor Angelo, "But his mother, brother and daughter are going to the surgery center, don't you think I should be there, too?" He looked at me with gentle eyes and said softly, "You love him, he is your husband, say goodbye now."

I thought, "You are right. I don't want to see this. I can't. I just want to say goodbye and remember him the way he looks right now, and then they can take him and do what they are going to do." He replied, "Wise choice, my dear."

One Night of Freedom

Pastor Angelo gave me the name of a funeral home and mortician. They have to remove the body once it is no longer alive. They take the body from the hospital. I had made those calls Sunday evening with Pastor Angelo's help because he said, "Look, this guy is my best friend. He's wonderful. That's who I want to take care of me when I'm gone." I agreed and called Trannino's Funeral Services.

Sunday night, Pastor Angelo and I stood side by side and gazed at my husband lying in his hospital bed. It was dark, and the flickering lights on the machines keeping Steve alive glimmered. I kissed Steve on the face, and I noticed he was still wearing his wedding band. I told Pastor Angelo, "I want that. I want his wedding band, please."

The nurses had to put oil on Steve's finger to slide it off because his hands were so swollen. I took the ring and put it in my handbag. Pastor Angelo and I prayed. We prayed together, and then I said my final goodbye to the father of my son, my best friend, my husband. With each step down the hospital corridor came excruciating pain. It felt like jolts of electricity were hitting every nerve in my body. I thought, "Oh, my God, I'm not going to make it. This is not happening. I'm never going to see him again on this earth. How do I go on? How do I "do" life now? I thought I would collapse.

I remember a sound starting in my belly and making its way up through my throat and out my mouth. What was this awful noise? Was someone being attacked? Did a mother just discover her child died? The God-awful sound was me. A guttural, primal scream from the deepest part of my being erupted. Jules and Kim were waiting for me in the waiting room. They heard me losing it, and they started crying; it was an awful night. I remember seeing Steve's family as I was leaving. They didn't look at me. They didn't talk to me. They stayed and went with Steve as they wheeled him into surgery. The last time I saw them (other than the funeral) was in the hospital, watching them follow Steve into the surgical center for the organ transplant.

I went home, and Jules stayed with me again that night. The next day, things began to get really interesting… as if they weren't already.

As I remember Steve's family during that long weekend, I mostly remember their remarkable lack of compassion, their lack of any human caring or sensitivity. That whole three-day weekend, Friday night, Saturday and Sunday, any interaction I had with them was not pleasant. It's almost like they were angry with me, but that's how they were for seven years. They never liked me. Doris just cried with her blood shot eyes and head buried in Kleenex, while Marion treated the whole situation like an internship for school. She actually said at one point, "I'm fascinated with the ICU care and Steve's medical protocol." Wow, talk about being cold hearted!

Johnathan, Steve's only living brother, the oldest son who is married to Marion, was very stone faced. However, that was his general persona. He didn't talk much. Sometimes, he wouldn't even look at me. For example, we would drive eight hours from Colorado with a screaming baby in the car to visit the family in Kansas, and he wouldn't even look me in the eye or say hello. How weird is that? None of this seemed shocking to him. He just stood there with absolutely no expression on his face.

In the hospital, the family was there fact finding. For example, "What exactly is that?" and "When can we do this," and "What time should we do that?" Steve was a human being. He wasn't someone's science project. It struck me as odd because my family is so vastly different. We are Italian. We emote over everything! Happy, sad, mad or glad, we emote in a big way!

I left the hospital for the last time on Sunday evening. The funeral service was scheduled for Thursday. The following Monday, Tuesday and Wednesday, the nightmare began.

CHAPTER 4

Wounded,
Still Breathing

Early Monday morning, I received news that my mother and sister were coming in from Texas. I asked Liz to pick up family members at the airport who were coming in for the funeral. I wasn't eating. I certainly wasn't sleeping, and I walked around with a constant ache in my stomach. I was attempting to get my finances in some semblance of order. I retrieved the piece of paper that Steve had printed up for me with names of banks, insurance companies, attorneys and key people I needed to contact. I was so incredibly afraid of being homeless. Money, to me, represented power and security. I was desperately afraid of being powerless and dependent on my family. I needed to secure some funds and find out what money existed for Jack and me to survive. As I was preparing to do that, two men, one named Don Allston (Steve's highest paid employee and friend) and another named Dick Richards (Steve's best friend and employee) came to my home and said, "Kate, we need to take all the computers out of here." I asked them, "Why? They're my computers." Don replied, "Well, there's a lot of top secret information on these computers." I asked, "You're not taking my personal computer, are you?" He said, "No. Not your laptop." But they took my other computer that wasn't a laptop, and it contained a lot of personal information like pictures, emails and my work stuff.

As they were removing the computers from my home, it was as if I wasn't even present. I became invisible. They stormed in, bulldozed past me, and took computers out of my house. I was stunned. This was one day after Steve had died.

Don Allston had been Steve's right-hand man at Latitude, Inc. I thought Don was a really nice guy, and I thought maybe he was the person I could lean on to help me do my life now. He seemed sincere and forthcoming. At the time, I was grateful for his assistance.

I started to make calls to the insurance companies and banks. I went down the list that Steve had given me. This list became my life line. As I made my way down this list, I discovered that some of the bank accounts Steve named were either closed or completely empty. Now I started to wonder, "My God, what if there are no insurance policies? What if this was all just a façade?" I called the largest insurance policy first. I told them my husband died. There was no compassion on the other end of the phone. They didn't say, "I'm so sorry to hear that. I'm sorry for your loss." They said, "When did he die? What did he die of? When we receive the proper forms from you, we will send a check." I remember feeling numb. I said the words, "My husband has just died," to every person named on that list. It seemed as if I was saying, "I'd like to buy the red sweater in this magazine." No one responded to my words regarding Steve's death. I didn't understand how some people presented with zero emotion.

I took notes, furious notes, on every phone call because my brain seemed to be on hold half the time. As I made each call, I listened as best I could and followed the directions I was given. Every time I dialed a number on that list, I braced myself for the response. Every life insurance company asked for a death certificate, copy of the obituary and a copy of my driver's license. I had to fill out every form perfectly. Each company had a different type of form, but I managed somehow to complete them all and mail them immediately. Even in my grief-stricken, exhausted state, I did what I had to do. I kept going down the list, making the next call and the next and the next.

I made fifteen calls, total, including those to the life insurance companies and seven to financial institutions of one type or another. Initially, I was getting answers like, "I'm sorry. That account is empty." That happened in the first two calls. I kept going down the list and then, with our local bank, where the business account was located, I was told I had $85,000 available to me. Out of the seven banks Steve listed, only two actually contained money.

As I went through everything, I discovered that Steve

lied about his financial situation. At some of the banks I called, the accounts had been closed for years. The realization that Steve deceived me intentionally was sickening. He had made the list only five or six months prior to his passing. I was in shock. I was angry and terribly sad. The questions that filled my brain were endless. Why would he lie? Why didn't he tell me everything about our financial situation?

Don Allston came to my house every day. I consulted him because I thought he was my friend. I'd ask him, "What do I do with this paper or this insurance policy? Did I fill this out correctly?" He reviewed everything. He'd say, "This looks good." He was one of the few people who knew exactly how much money I was going to receive. He mailed some of the forms for me overnight. He was very helpful in many ways. Little did I know at the time, Don had ulterior motives. He was motivated by greed and selfishness.

Don suggested we go to the Credit Union, the bank that had a portion of Steve's money. I had no way of accessing this money because Steve had never put my name on the account. Don asked, "Kate, I know you're in shock and going through a great deal, but can you pull yourself together enough to accompany me to this bank?" This was one day before my husband's funeral and two days after my husband's death.

I got dressed up and looked as nice as I possibly could. I remember I wore cream colored dress pants (that barely hung on my body with a belt) and a cream-colored blouse (the opposite color of grief clothing). We went to the bank, DS Credit Union, with Steve's death certificate. We walked in, and Don said, "Hi. We need to see someone regarding this type of an account." The woman we were speaking to said, "Well, who are you?" She was very rude and snippy. I started to break down because I was so raw, and this woman had no compassion toward my situation. Don said, "Look, her husband just died two days ago." She looked at both of us oddly and quickly replied, "Oh, you need the decedent specialist." She never offered me water, a tissue or even a smile. I got her name and her business card. It was good that I kept it. It would be of use to me down the road.

The decedent specialist, Jacob, came out. He explained to me very matter-of-factly that they would freeze all my accounts if I didn't pay the one credit card that Steve had taken out through their bank. I remember sitting there with Don in the meeting, feeling more hopeless by the second. I started to cry and said, "Why would you do that? That savings account is mine. It's mine, even though my name isn't on it, that's my money. It's all I have to live off until these policies start to come to fruition." He replied coldly, "Well, I'm sorry but that's just how it is."

I kept thinking about the $85,000 in the business account for Latitude. I had complete access to it but was trying not to touch it because I didn't know if that was appropriate. I quietly said to Jacob, "Look, I will pay off that credit card, just please don't freeze those accounts." I begged him, begged him, "Please don't." He said, "Well, we'll give you a little bit of time, due to the circumstances."

Apparently, I had to pay off some credit card Steve had acquired through their bank, or they would freeze the account. This particular account was all the money I had earned from the gym. It's what I had to live off until some life insurance policy came through. I also became the new owner and president of Latitude Inc. the minute Steve passed way. Don was coming over each day and saying, "I'll help you with this. I'll help you with whatever I can." He said, "Look, when one of these policies comes through, I don't know which one will come through first, but I'd like you to give Latitude Inc. $50,000." I said, "I'm sorry, what?" I couldn't believe he was asking me for money.

I said, "Why would I give the company money when I can't even walk through the door because I don't have a clearance? Why would I give $50,000 to a company that you're telling me is struggling? Why would I do that? This is money for my son and me that Steve planned for our future." Don said, "Kate, you have to do something. You're the owner of the company. It would really help a lot." I answered, "Right. Okay. I see what you're saying." I didn't say no right away. I appeased him and said, "I'll think about it."

Steve paid himself every two weeks. I remember it

was somewhere in the realm of $10,000 every two weeks that would go into our bank account. Steve died on the 6th of April and on the 15th of each month, he got paid. I asked Don if Steve would be receiving his paycheck on April 15th because we needed it desperately! I needed to pay the mortgage and the other bills that were ominously close to their due dates. He replied casually, "You know what, Kate? I don't think we're going to have Steve's paycheck deposited." I said, "Well, why? You guys are paid. He made sure you all got paid. Why wouldn't you pay his widow and son and deposit his paycheck that he worked for?" He said, "Well, you know, it's one of those things. We're just not really sure how the payroll's working out now. Steve's not here." I said, "But his wife and child are very much still here." I started to see a side of Don that sent a chill up my spine. He was very selfish. He was mean and insensitive. He was a fraud through and through. I was extremely nervous about Don. He was helping me fill out paperwork but asking for lots of money. Is this why he was helping me? I prayed for guidance and wisdom.

I went to Colorado Bank upon the advice of the attorney who drew up Steve's will. When I called him, he said, "Kate, I want you to go to that bank. Take out $10,000 cash and hide it. Don't tell anybody. Just go do that now!" He also said, "Don is a son of a bitch, and I don't know why he's acting this way, but people can be very greedy." This lawyer was a very nice gentleman. He told me, "You're entitled to it. You own the company. It's your money." Now, looking back, I wish I had taken his advice.

There was a woman at our local bank named Kiki. She had my back. She saw that every time I went to the bank, Don was with me. He was always looking over my shoulder. He knew my passcodes. He knew everything there was to know about Steve's finances. Kiki pulled me aside and said, "Can I speak with you, Kate, privately?" I said, "Sure." She said, "What's going on?" I asked, "What's up?" I explained to her, "Don's just helping me." She shook her head emphatically, "No, he isn't. He's bulldozing you, and you need to stop this. It's okay for you to come here by yourself. I will have your best interest at heart. I loved your husband. He was a great guy, and I think you're great as well."

I started crying and hugged her. She was a strong woman, and I really liked her brutal honesty. She helped me and gave me the courage to tell Don to go pound sand. I started to think about the people who worked for Steve. I was always so concerned about their bonus checks and holiday parties. I wanted Steve to be a generous, godly leader. However, some of the employees didn't respect me, and I'm not sure why. One of the guys who worked with Steve once told me, "You know, Kate, when we first met you, we thought you were Steve's trophy wife. I thought Steve was getting his freak on." I looked at him with eyes that could kill. I wanted to punch him in the face. I thought to myself, "I'm not fifteen or twenty years younger than Steve. I have a Master's Degree in Clinical Counseling. I'm an educated, God-fearing woman. I wasn't just arm candy, and it wasn't okay for him to say that. I believe some of them thought I was with Steve because he had money. It was disturbing, knowing some of my late husband's employees thought I was simply another acquisition of his.

I spoke to the funeral director that Pastor Angelo recommended on Sunday, and we met Monday evening. My mother and sister were with me when Mr. Trannino from the funeral home arrived. It was in Steve's will that he wished to be cremated. One of the toughest conversations you can ever have in life, is discussing your dead spouse's body and what to do with it. The mortician had a cold, stone face. He showed very little emotion, and his affect was flat. I guess when you work with grieving families and dead people for a living, this happens. He resembled Ricardo Montalban, the handsome actor from Fantasy Island. He had a Spanish accent and dark, penetrating eyes. He casually asked me, "Kate, what do you want? Do you want this kind of box or this kind...?" I shrieked, "Box? What do you mean?" My mother interjected, "Just go with the cardboard." I screamed, "Mom! No, I'm not putting my husband in just anything! He was my husband, my best friend, a real person." I was crying and had a brutal headache from all the emotional turmoil. What I did not know at the time, was that a person must be contained in something before cremation. Anyway, we discussed all the details, and the bottom line was it was going to cost $4,000 to cremate Steve, buy the container and the urn for his remains. Four thousand dollars I did not have! I had funds, but I didn't want to spend them because I'd be using the money for the mortgage and bills to pay for the cremation. Even though I knew money would be coming in, I didn't have access to it at that moment. This was a dilemma. My sister, Drew, mentioned, "You know those credit cards Steve has," (they were all still open). She continued, "Let's call. Let's find out what he owes or if there's any credit left on any of them."

So, my brave, attorney sister started making calls. Drew stood about 5'4 (on a good day) with flaxen chestnut colored hair and chocolate doe eyes. Her skin was not olive toned like mine; it was much more pale and luminescent. My sister is a beautiful, very bright woman. I have the utmost respect for her for a thousand reasons! Drew was able to reach the first card we called. She spoke to the woman on the other end, pretending to be me, Kate Williams. She said, "Look, I need your help. From one woman to another." This is how my sister approached the situation; she used emotional pain to tap into the woman's empathy. The woman said, "You know what? Even though I know Steve's dead, nobody I work for knows that he's dead. I'm going to let you make this one charge, and then we'll shut it down." Drew said, "Thank you, thank you from the bottom of my heart." I loved my sister for this. I gave the mortician the credit card information. I said, "Look, that's all you can charge, just the amount you mentioned." This is how the funeral, cremation, obituary and death certificates were paid.

Don advised me not to pay my mortgage. I replied, "Don, I'm not going to do that. I need to pay this mortgage." I'm anal retentive about paying bills. If a bill comes in, I'll write a check and put it in the mail. It doesn't even go on my desk. It just goes back out the door with a check. Don half chuckling said, "You know, Kate, you need to call the mortgage company and tell them Steve passed away. They will be lenient and understanding and let this month's payment ride. They'll simply tack it on the end." He repeated, "Tell them your husband died, and they'll be compassionate. They'll tack it on at the end and let you slide for this month." I didn't feel comfortable doing that. I needed to know that at least my house was secure. For another thirty days, I could still live in my home and not worry. So, on the first of May, I paid the mortgage.

Basically, during the three days before the funeral, there were a lot of financial issues and tons of paperwork to sort out. There were the men coming to take the computers out and Don advising me not to pay the mortgage and saying, "Hey, could you give the company $50,000 when you get some money?" (He was a real piece of work.)

The mortician also came over during that three-day

period. We had to plan the funeral. I had to choose the songs. I had to find a picture for the Mass card and the obituary. I had to choose the type of Mass card I wanted and what song, hymn or quote to place on one side of the card. It was crazy to have to make these decisions in a time of feeling completely disconnected to reality. Your brain is not functioning normally. You're flying by the seat of your pants.

People knew to call Pastor Angelo because he was the contact name in the newspaper. He was getting calls from all over the place, even Colombia. I planned the entire memorial service. I told Pastor Angelo that I would give Steve's eulogy. We asked Samantha, his daughter, "Do you want to say something?" She said, "Yes, I'd like to say something, but Kate, you, of course, will go first as his wife." We asked his brother, Johnathan, "Do you want to say anything?" He said, "No, no. I can't talk." It was myself and Steve's daughter, Samantha, who would speak at the memorial service. I believe my eulogy was perfect. I didn't choke. I didn't cry. I had some tears, but I was very clear. I wanted people to hear what I had to say about this man; he deserved that. I wanted people to know the truth about how good Steve was as a man, husband and father. I wanted everyone to know he was a champion. Champions fall in love with discomfort, and Steve was uncomfortable every day. I cried afterwards.

The service was held at Calvary Chapel. It was jam-packed with people from all over the United States. Jack was only five at the time. He broke down once in the beginning of the service when videos of me, Steve and himself were being shown. Although I was wearing a body skimming black dress and 3-inch heels, I scooped Jack up into my arms tightly. My little boy was undone. He was confused, scared and simply undone.

Steve's favorite bands were Pink Floyd and Queen. They were playing his favorite songs, and Jack recognized them. They showed a video of us as a family. The pictures of us were on the screen as the songs played, and Jack looked at me and burst into tears. That's why I picked him up quickly and walked to the front of the church. I held him in my arms, shushing him like he was a baby and rocked back and forth with my little golden boy in my arms. After some time, I heard Pastor Angelo's resounding voice. He was talking about Steve and myself and how involved with the church we both were. He mentioned Steve's tenacity, generosity and warm heart. Then, he asked me to approach the podium and speak. I wasn't nervous. I had written down on paper exactly what I wanted to say. I spoke about Steve's love of his children, his wife and his family. I also spoke of my husband's bravery and courage battling ALS. It was not verbose or long winded. After I spoke, Samantha spoke. I remember thinking, "What in the name of heaven is she wearing???" Her dress was way too short for a funeral, and her shoes looked like something from my granny's attic! Oh well, no time for the fashion police, it's a funeral! We had a luncheon afterwards, so families could gather and reminisce. Steve always told me, "Honey, go somewhere cool and have some drinks. Don't just sit around and cry about me, go somewhere you like to go." I told him emphatically I would, that I would absolutely honor his request.

Boy, I was tapped out. I had just spent the credit card for the funeral, but I scheduled the luncheon, anyway. I chose a local Italian restaurant for the luncheon. My sister said she would pay for it if there were no other options. We both wanted to have something nice where family and friends could go and relax and talk. That was what Steve had wanted.

Steve's brother, Johnathan, is a millionaire, actually a multi-millionaire. He works in hedge funds and financial consulting. Marion, his wife, had just graduated nursing school with her RN degree. My mother suggested, "Why don't you ask Johnathan to pay for the luncheon? You paid for the funeral. Why don't you ask Johnathan to pay for the luncheon?" All the people present were mostly Steve's family, not mine. They were folks from Kansas that I had never even met before. I said, "Mom, I can't do it. You do it." She went to Marion, the evil witch, and said, "Hey, Marion, Kate's really strapped for money right now. Could you guys spring for the luncheon?"

Marion said, "Well, that's ridiculous. Steven (she always called Steve, Steven. No one else did, just her), Steven showed us his finances and said Kate will have tons of money. She'll never have to worry." My mother said, "No, no. Not right now. We're not there, yet." My mom and Marion were a perfect match because my mom's tough as nails. She said, "No, Marion. That's not the case now, and my daughter doesn't lie. So, will you pay for the luncheon or not?" Marion wouldn't answer. My sister, Drew, said, "I'll pay for the damn lunch. Don't worry about it." I said, "Drew, I don't want you to do that." I felt bad. Finally, after going around and around, Johnathan agreed to pay for the luncheon.

Nobody from Steve's side of the family was speaking with us. There were seven long tables. My mom, my sister, and a few close friends of mine were at one table. The other six were filled with relatives I've never met.

I used to like Steve's Uncle Danny. He was a football coach of a college that did really well in football for years. He was a handsome, cool guy. You could see why he made an excellent coach. He and I always got along well. We would laugh and talk and have a great time when we visited Kansas, and he was there. He came up to me and said, "I'm sorry for your loss," and walked quickly away.

For the life of me, I have no idea why Steve's family never really liked me and pretended for seven years. I knew Marion hated my guts, but as for the rest of the people, I thought I had won them over. Patricia, Steve's mom's sister, came up to me and said, "You have the most darling figure." That's exactly what she said. I'm thinking,

"Thanks?" How about "How are you doing?" It was bizarre, surreal.

When the luncheon was over, I was walking to my car with my mom and sister when Marion came rushing out after me panting, "I want a copy of the eulogy! You must get me copy! It was amazing, simply beautiful." She threw her arms around me and hugged me. I was flabbergasted.

My theory is, Marion's dramatic demonstration of affection and praise toward me was all a big show for the entire family. She made a big scene of hugging me and being nice to me (which never happened), so that everyone present could witness her kindness. Jonathan, Steve's older brother said to me quietly, "Hey, when Jack gets a little older, if he has questions about his father, I would like to be the one to talk to him." I looked at him and said, "Really? You would do that?" This made me think we would be staying in touch with each other. It was a lovely gesture. I said, "Thanks, Johnathan. I love you." I always said I love you to them.

As I began the drive back to my house, with my mother and sister in the car, the strangest thing occurred. I couldn't remember how to get to my house. My house is only three miles from the church. I was disoriented and confused. Nothing appeared the same. Houses, street signs and neighborhoods I had seen for eight years living in Colorado all looked strange. My sister finally spoke up and said, "Hey Sis, would you like me to drive?" I paused and said, "No, I've got it, we'll be home shortly." I guess

I was in some sort of shock." I'll Map Quest the address, and it will be fine," I assured her. I was completely disoriented. I finally got us home safely and we all collapsed in our rooms for several hours.

After the funeral, Steve's family came by the house before leaving for Kansas. I will never forget the words Marion spoke to me as we gathered in the kitchen. She boldly asked, "Oh, have you heard from the organ donor people at Alliance?" I said, "No." She said, "Well, I think they used Steve's retinas, too. They took his eyes." In that moment, I wanted to dive over the counter and strangle her with my bare hands. If ever I were going to commit murder, that would have been the day. I felt like I wanted to vomit. When she said that, all I could picture was Steve's face without eyes. That's the vision that flashed inside my head over and over. I felt like my insides were imploding and I was going to pass out. The room was spinning, and I couldn't focus on anything. My mother witnessed the entire conversation and said firmly, "Marion, I need to speak to you. Would you come with me into the other room, please?" All I said to her was, "No, No, they didn't do that. No, just the kidney. That's it." My mother told Marion to never, ever bring up the organ donation subject again with me. She firmly suggested that Marion attempt to be kind and empathic with me during this time. I spoke with Doris and said, "How are you doing?" I was concerned for her. This was her second son who died relatively young. She said, "Oh, Katie." She just kept shaking her head. She looked like Mrs. Claus. She was so cute. I said, "I'm so sorry, mom." I used to call her mom. It just felt natural. I called her mom all the time. I said, "I'm sorry, mom." I hugged her and repeated, "You're going to get through this. You're going to be okay. We're all going to be okay." They stayed maybe an hour, to an hour-and-a-half and then left. That day was the last time I've ever seen them.

Except for Samantha and Martin, I never heard from any of the family again. Not a card, note, email, text or S.O.S message from any of them. My family also left and returned to Houston. It was just little Jack and me in this gigantic, silent house.

I couldn't go back to work immediately because every day, from the time Steve died until after the funeral and for weeks after that, I was constantly in a meeting. I had to meet with attorneys, banks, and other financial institutions daily. There was always some document, affidavit or contract that needed my signature.

It seemed the only people who cared that I was hurting were my gym family. They are my best friends. My boss, Mike, came to my house and brought Jack and me dinner on several occasions. He texted me every day. He would say, "Keep breathing and keep moving one day at a time. It's all you've got to do, Kate. Just inhale, exhale, repeat." He'd also say, "Eat a damn burger once in a while, would you?" I was so skinny, it was scary. I looked waif like and gaunt. My weight had plummeted to a whopping 110 pounds. (And I'm 5'8).

Jack went back to school immediately. Jack was only five and in first grade. He had completed kindergarten and preschool at a Christian academy. I'd walk him in every day, and as I was walking, I felt eyes on me. The stares were almost painful. I could feel the women's eyes burning through my flesh at times. I thought, "What is wrong with these Stepford wives?" They all looked the same; overweight, matronly women with hair pulled into a messy pony tail donned in sweat pants. I didn't exactly fit the mold! I was covered in tattoos from head to toe, thin as a rail and wore jeans and vintage t-shirts most days.

I contacted a therapist for some counseling for Jack. She was an MFT (marriage and family therapist) and had another degree in art therapy. She specialized in children who were grieving. Jack had definitely been traumatized by the loss of his father. Jack thought if he got sick or hurt himself, he could go see his dad in heaven. I told him, "No honey, it doesn't work that way." This is why I was terribly concerned and found a therapist immediately. This therapist's name was Celia. She was a petite redhead with lots of spunk. Once a week, we took Jack to therapy with Miss Celia.

Sue and Dick came over for Easter. They came over for a few hours, we had a small ham, and they left. Jack's birthday fell on Mother's Day weekend. There was no card, no present, nothing for him from Steve's family. Every year like clockwork, Marion would send a gift for Jack. They treated Jack pretty well while Steve was alive. As soon as Steve died, that all changed. They didn't even acknowledge Jack's existence, let alone mine.

CHAPTER 5

Happy Birthday

Steve died on April 6th and my birthday happens to be April 19th. I had made plans months before Steve passed to go out with my girlfriends. I paid for a limousine to come pick us up and take us all to dinner. We were going to a quaint little restaurant called Lacotta and then dancing at a local club called the W. It wasn't an "everyone 21 to 30, bumping and grinding, doing shots" kind of place. It was a small bar and restaurant that showcased amazing bands. The bands were absolutely mind blowing. One band called Hot Stuff was my favorite. They played old school music from the seventies and eighties. The age range at the W was thirty to sixty. So, the plan was to eat and drink and dance the night away. My girlfriends and I could have a few drinks and not worry about driving, hence the prepaid limousine.

When you are a full- time caregiver, it's important to make time for fun things or "me" time. It helps you keep your sanity and prevent depression. I had made plans to go out for my birthday months prior. I planned this event to lift me up a little bit and give me something to look forward to. Steve was more than happy to have me go out and have a good time with my girlfriends. However, I had no idea Steve was going to die on April 6th. I thought I should cancel the birthday plans because it was so soon after his passing. What will people think? What if someone I know sees me out dancing and drinking? I'd be cast as the widow who wasn't home grieving and crying but out on the town partying! I said to Elizabeth, "I can't go out, it's so inappropriate. What will people think? God forbid I'm not the weeping widow." She shook her head and replied, "Kate, you need this, and you're going out. You're going to celebrate your birthday with the women who love you." She actually said, "Screw what people think; this is about you. This is your birthday, and we have plans."

I thought, "Okay, I'll follow through, but let's not do the dinner thing. Let's just meet at my house. We'll have the limo come around 8:00 pm. We'll go out for a couple of hours and come home." Liz smiled and said, "Great." So, the five of us prepared for our evening of laughter and dancing. I decided to wear a little red dress that I had bought in Austin, Texas when I was there with my sisters. It was a designer dress that looked amazing on my figure. I was so thin, anything I put on looked great. The material of this dress was like workout clothing and stretched with you. It was backless with skinny spaghetti straps that came up over the shoulders. It was very sexy. I threw on a pair of my high-heeled "going out" shoes and suddenly became a six-foot-tall dancing queen. I applied my makeup carefully and ran a brush through my hair. I used a bit of hairspray to add drama to my look. As I looked in the mirror, I thought, "Okay, I guess I look acceptable." My girlfriends came over with smiles and gifts for me. The limo arrived promptly at 8:00pm and took us to the W.

I will never forget what happened the minute I walked into that bar. I was laughing with my girlfriend Kylie, a beautiful, curvy brunette when I felt eyes burning through me. I turned to see who was staring at me. I spotted two gentlemen standing by the bar. One was shorter, with broad shoulders and a devastating smile, and the other was tall and a bit older with salt and pepper hair and a friendly face. The guy with the amazing shoulders and awesome smile was pointing at me with his finger motioning for me to come to him. I thought, "This isn't happening. Is he pointing at me?" The band was playing, "Brick House" and I thought, "God, I can't believe I'm here." I took a deep breath and walked over to the gorgeous man pointing at me and motioning with his finger for me to come to him. As I got closer, I noticed how truly beautiful his face was. He had high cheek bones, full lips and eyes that looked right through me. He had on a black bolero hat, faded jeans and a crisp black shirt that was tight enough to see the defined muscles of his back and shoulders. I approached him slowly, like a doe learning to walk for the first time. He looked at me and

Happy Birthday

asked, "You wanna dance?" I said, "Sure," and we headed to the dance floor. We started dancing, and I realized the last time I had danced with a man was five years ago at a wedding with Steve. Steve and I had attended a lovely wedding in Estes Park. One of Steve's employees, Alicia, was tying the knot. We danced our faces off at that reception! Anyway, I discovered the gentleman's name was Hunter, Hunter Ridge. I thought to myself, "Of course his name is Hunter, that's probably what he's doing here!" We danced and moved together the entire evening. It felt so good to move my body to music and have a handsome man telling me how pretty I was. Hunter would look at me and say, "You're so pretty." He must have said it one hundred times. I was flattered by his compliments and simply said thank you.

I told him bluntly, "Look, my husband just died, literally just died. I'm crazy. I'm not okay." He replied softly, "That's okay." He continued, "If you need someone to talk to, a shoulder, I will listen." I thought, "Is he just saying this to get me into bed? Does he mean this? Could he be as nice as he appears at this moment?" Hunter told me he was divorced almost seven years and single for the past eleven months. He explained he had broken up with his girlfriend almost one year ago. He also told me he owned his own Welding Company called Rock Welding. As the evening drew to an end, I felt excited, scared and extremely tired. I decided to give Hunter my phone number. We awkwardly exchanged numbers and said good bye. He told me he would call me soon.

Hunter called the next day, which happened to be my birthday. We made a plan to see each other on Monday evening, three days after our initial meeting. I kept thinking to myself, "What in the hell am I doing? Is this ok? What if he's some kind of freak?" I was terribly nervous and anxious for his arrival. Knowing Hunter was coming to my house eased my grief. It was like a cooling salve to a bloodied wound. I could breathe normally again for a minute. I decided to wear jeans, a tank top and long sweater. I thought my outfit said, "I'm a stylish yet sexy mom."

Hunter decided to ride his Harley to my house. He came over on his bike, and it was extremely loud. I thought, "Oh my God, what are the neighbors going to think?" This was bad because a motorcycle would draw attention. I said, "Do you really have to ride that thing? Can't you just use your car?" He said, "Well, it's nice weather." It was April, and it was getting warmer. I said, "Okay, whatever, who cares what the neighbors think, anyway." We sat in my family room and talked. He told me about his daughters and ex-wife and ex-girlfriend, and I told him about my husband's death.

I cried a lot. I said, "I can't believe this is happening to me. I can't believe this is my life." Then we talked about other things, fun things like music and movies. I remember when he sat close to me, I got a chill up my spine and almost couldn't breathe. He was so manly. He had that Sam Elliot kind of a thing going on. His voice was very deep, and I absolutely adored his southern accent. When he covered my hand with his, it was as if an electric shock ran through my entire body. My blood turned into melted butter running through my veins. I could smell his cologne. It reminded me of the woods on a crisp fall day. I was mesmerized by his voice. He had such a deep, guttural voice. When he spoke, I had no idea what he was saying. I just stared at his full, red, luscious mouth. While he spoke, I was wondering what his mouth would feel like on mine. Would he kiss me? How would he kiss me? It had been so long since I was physical with anyone, it was like I was obsessed. I never thought I would meet someone this soon. It had only been 12 days since Steve died. I told Jack, "Hey, this is a friend of mommy's." I didn't say anything ridiculous like, "Hi, this is your new step-dad." I explained to Hunter that Jack had a rough time while Steve was ill. I explained that I was worried how Jack would respond to a new guy on the scene. I didn't know what to do. Was Jack going be okay? Is he scarred for life? I was concerned. So, Hunter and I discussed each other's children and how best to introduce them to each other. We agreed Hunter's girls would come to Jack's 6th birthday party. Jack was turning six in three weeks. Hunter and I continued to see each other. He came over almost every day. I appreciated this so much because when I was in his presence, I felt almost normal. I didn't have my sister or my mom or my mother-in-law staying with me to help. My girlfriends were preoccupied with their own lives. I remember asking Jules and Sue, my two besties, to alternate spending nights with me. The thought of being alone was terrifying. My pain was palpable. It was as if pain became my new roommate. I was learning how to live with it ever present. I recalled a hot yoga class I had taken years back. The instructor kept saying," Ladies, find a place to rest in the pain." That's exactly what I was doing. I moved with pain, danced with pain and slept with pain. It was my constant companion. With only Jack and me in this humongous house, the house actually echoed! Hunter's presence definitely filled a void.

Hunter worked during the day and then would shower at his house and drive over to my house. His house was about forty-five minutes away from mine. Sometimes, he arrived at 7:00, 8:00, or 9:00 pm. I'd have something for him to eat, and we would just talk, or watch a movie, or do something. This went on for two or three months, maybe three or four times a week.

One night when he came over, he said, "I'm really tired." I replied, "Well, you don't have to drive home. That's crazy, you can just stay here." I continued, "Look, I haven't been with a man in three years. No one has touched me. I have lived without the touch or caress of a loving husband for years. I said, "I'm a Christian woman. I can't sleep with you. I can't." He answered, "Yes, you can, you definitely can." I just started laughing. We were sitting on the sofa, and Jack fell asleep. I put Jack to bed and kissed his beautiful, golden head. I remember sitting there next to Hunter when he reached for me hungrily. I was so taken aback, I didn't resist. His mouth was hot and wet and eagerly searching mine. I felt feverish and confused. The feelings of desire that had been buried for years sprang to life when he touched me. I felt slight and vulnerable around him. For the first time in years, I felt like a woman, feminine and beautiful. I had been a robot for so many years. This was almost too much emotion for me to handle at one time.

We progressed from the couch to the bedroom. He was so gentle with me, like I was a china doll. He told me I appeared fragile to him, and he handled me like a glass ornament he didn't want to break. I was so nervous and scared. At one point, I blurted out, "I can't do it; this is wrong." Finally, while listening to Hunter's reassuring and comforting words, I surrendered. Being in his arms was the medicine I needed desperately.

My true friends knew that the past few years had been extremely difficult, and I was sad. Even my boss said to me, "You smile now. You smile all the time." He said, "It's so good to see that, Kate." I started to put my weight back on and have a figure. I was so scrawny, it was horrible. I was coming to life again, just starting to bloom in a new way. My friends were very excited. They were happy for me. I explained to them, "Hey, I met someone, and we're kind of hanging out. I don't want to date other people, just him." They were all stoked.

My pastor, on the other hand, Pastor Angelo, whom I had known for over seven years, said (and this is a conversation I'll never forget) that what Hunter and I were doing was disgusting. He continued to tell me that I was disgusting in the eyes of the Lord.

Pastor Angelo was the pastor of the local church I attended. Steve had requested in his will that Pastor Angelo perform his memorial service. Pastor Angelo was there at the hospital with me on the last night of Steve's life. He would call me once a week to say, "Hey, how are you doing?" On one of those calls, I said, "Hey, I met someone, and I'm really feeling happy. I feel alive again. I feel like there's hope for a future." He said, "Well, he's not living with you, is he?" I said, "No, not yet." I continued, "We're talking about it because he wants to sell his house anyway, and this house is huge, plenty of room." He said, "Well, let me just say this, if you've been physical with him, or if you've been sexual, it's disgusting in the eyes of God. God looks at that behavior as an abomination." When I heard those words fall out of his mouth, it was as if I had been punched hard in the stomach and couldn't breathe. I have loved the Lord for many, many years. I have taught Sunday school, played on the Worship Team and acted as a lector on various occasions. I know what the Bible says about promiscuity, adultery and marriage. "Wow, that's a really strong statement," I replied. He said,

Happy Birthday

"Kate, I need to tell you the truth. I can't sugar coat it or water it down." I hung up. I have never spoken to Pastor Angelo since. I have not been back to that church and have no plans of going back ever.

My mother and sisters also voiced, "I think it's too soon for you to be involved with anyone." I said to my mother, "Walk a day in my shoes, one day, then you can judge me. I don't want to hear it, mom." I continued, "Unless you have something positive to say, don't talk to me." I told my family that I grieved Steve long before he actually died because he was gone long before he died. He was a shadow of himself. It wasn't like he died in a car accident, suddenly. My sister Drew said, "Don't you think it's too soon? What about Jack… Blah, blah." I told her vehemently, "Jack and Hunter get along great. It's good for Jack. He's playing ball. He's outside playing catch. We're not calling him dad. I'm not getting married. We're just seeing each other, getting to know each other. I'm not going to date a whole bunch of people. I don't want to do that." Drew said, "Wow, I totally get it. I am so sorry, Katie. You suffered for so long, you deserve some happiness. Can't wait to meet him." The Steve they knew was long gone before he actually died. She continued, "Kate, I understand, and I am so very happy for you." I was relieved and happy that my sister, Drew, understood. It was important to me that my family accept Hunter.

I had enrolled Jack in a Christian elementary school. He was in kindergarten, going into first grade. Every day you had to walk the kindergartners into the school. When Steve was alive, he insisted on trying to walk from the parking lot with Jack in tow, to the entrance of the school. It took forever. There was ice, snow, and everybody watched. Everybody saw us, the mom who was a trainer, the sick husband, and the beautiful, golden little boy. Every day, we did this. Then one day I said to Steve, "I don't think you should attempt walking Jack into the school anymore. If you slip, it could be catastrophic!" He insisted on driving with me to the school, but he promised he wouldn't get out of the car. We did this every day for months. One Monday morning bright and early, Hunter said, "I'd like to go with you today to take Jack to school." I thought, "Uh oh, this could be disastrous, but why not?" No one knew who Hunter was in relation to me. He could have been my brother, cousin, or friend. They certainly didn't know any intimate details! Hunter has a lot of tattoos; he's sleeved. He is a very imposing figure. He's the kind of guy who walks into a room and heads turn. We decided to walk Jack into the school together.

We both exited the vehicle, and I grabbed little Jack's arm to guide him. We made it up the stairs and through the entrance. So far, so good. Then it happened. A group of moms and several teachers were gathered in the hallway chatting when they spotted us. Their eyes nearly popped out of their heads. Their jaws dropped to the floor, and they were rendered speechless. They stared at us like we each had two heads! I thought to myself, 'They are probably thinking, 'There's that slutty mom and her sleeved boyfriend in our Christian academy!'" What really made me angry was that they took it out on Jack. I would get a call almost every day, "Oh, he threw a pencil. Oh, he forgot his notebook etc...." I replied with sharp sarcasm, "You're kidding me, right?" I screamed, "His father just died! He threw a pencil, and he's in the principal's office? Why am I not in the principal's office with my son?" The principal of the school was a strange man. He looked like a singer in a Mariachi band. He had olive skin with a mustache that curled up on each end. He rarely said hello to anyone and mostly kept to himself. He was the kind of guy that gives you the creeps. I called him immediately when I discovered Jack was in the office alone with him being chastised for the most abominable crime; pencil tossing!

A few similar incidents occurred during the following weeks. One teacher actually had the nerve to ask me what my relationship with Hunter was all about! She nosily inquired, "What is the exact nature of your relationship with Hunter?" I told her, "It's none of your business. Who I'm dating is no one's business but my own. I'm paying a thousand dollars a month for my son to attend this school. I'm basically paying your salary, lady." She snootily replied, "Well, actually Kate, your relationship is our business. The academy is represented by wholesome, God-fearing families." I responded angrily, "You know what? I'm done here! You never took an interest in me when my husband was alive. Now, all of a sudden, you're interested in my life? You're a hypocrite!" I stomped off with tears in my eyes.

Kindergarten graduation was around the corner. I was so proud of little Jack! The school asked that we buy a white, buttoned-down men's Oxford shirt for the kids to wear over their clothes. They provided the black graduation cap and tassel. I was confused at first, but then when I put the shirt on Jack, it looked like a robe! As much as I hated the school, it was an ingenious idea! We got Jack dressed and ready for his big day! He looked so stinking cute, I couldn't stand it! "What a beautiful boy God has given me," I thought. Once at the school, the kids had to go with their teacher and stand in formation on the stage. I sat in the audience with Hunter, Elizabeth and Grace (another girlfriend who sometimes helped me with Jack). We all watched eagerly as the ceremony began. The kids sang songs and received their diplomas. The Principal of the Early Education Grades, Mr. Don, called Jack's name and handed him his diploma with a brimming smile. Although the graduation was lovely, I noticed something peculiar. No one spoke to me. Not one parent or teacher said one single word to me. I thought to myself, my husband died six weeks ago, does anyone care? Does anyone have a heart here?

I made a decision to pull Jack out of this so-called Christian Academy. After his graduation, I put him in the public school only two minutes from the house. He loved it, and I loved it. They're warm; they're friendly; they're kind, so different!

Part of the reason I didn't feel guilty about my relationship with Hunter was that it just happened. He had been out of a relationship for over a year. He was at the W that night and was thinking, "This place sucks, and I'm leaving," and then I walked in with my girlfriends. He thought, "Wait, I'm going to stay for a minute or two. Let's check this out. We both were not looking for a relationship. God works in mysterious ways!

Steve and I had a very serious talk one day about four or five weeks before he died. He said, "Look, this conversation is going to be hard. It's almost impossible for me to say what I'm about to say, but it needs to be said. I need you to promise me to continue to live. I want you to live. Jack needs a dad, and I don't want you to feel like I'm watching you and thinking, "I can't believe she's with another man already." He continued, "You're a beautiful woman, Kate; you're full of life. You've got to go on." I replied, choking back tears, "No. Don't die, you can't die yet." I kept repeating, "Please don't die. Please don't leave me!" This conversation ran through my brain, over and over again. Steve wanted me to go on. He wanted me to live. I decided to honor his request.

Another salve I used for the pain was travel. We went away a lot. I even considered moving to Miami. I traveled as much as I possibly could. I rented a house in Miami for six months. We went to Miami in June, and in July we visited San Diego, California. It was so much fun. We stayed at the Del Coronado on Coronado Island. It was simply magical! A couple of months after this trip, we were back in Miami. Being away, in a different location, seemed to ease the pain.

Hunter knew that there were complications with Latitude, Inc. I met him in April, and from that time forward, he knew I owned Steve's company. He knew I was trying to sell it and that I was looking for a way, praying, "Please God, I've got to sell this company. I can't own it. I can't even walk into the building. This is crazy." Hunter was saying, "Well, I'll run it." But I replied, "Honey, you don't understand. You don't have a degree in geospatial, whatever it's called, mapping. You're not a cartographer or a geographer." I continued, "I appreciate the thought, but I don't think that would be a good idea." Finally, after asking everyone I knew if they knew anyone in this area of expertise, I found someone! I met the gentleman through a life-long friend of mine named Lane. Lane was a tall blond. She stood about 6 ft. tall and could be referred to as a "tall drink of water." She moved to Miami from D.C. about twelve years prior and was renting her house for income while she lived in an apartment on the beach.

She had worked for the government for years and made many connections. Mitch Halliday was one of those connections. He had been in the military for over thirty years. He was a retired, highly decorated officer. In his retirement, he decided to buy and sell government related companies. Lane told me she thought Mitch was the perfect guy to buy Latitude, Inc. So, one day I called him and said, "Hey, I'm Kate Williams, the current owner of Latitude. I have no idea what I'm doing as far as this company is concerned. I need to sell it, and my close friend Lane recommended you highly. Can we talk about this?" My initial conversation with Mitch took place in May, one month after Steve's death. Mitch said he was very interested in my proposition to buy the company. We set a date to meet and discuss logistics. I was so relieved and hopeful at the prospect of unloading this albatross.

The only thing I got from Latitude was pounding headaches. Don had asked me for $50,000 to help the credit card situation. It seemed as though the company was drowning. However, I did not know this for certain. Because Don was constantly asking me for money, I assumed Latitude was low on cash flow. Mitch had suggested we meet at a local restaurant for lunch. I chose Outback because it was close, casual and had food I could eat. I arrived at the restaurant first and reserved a booth for us. Mitch was on time to the very minute. I knew it was him before he introduced himself. Mitch stood about 6'3" and was dressed in a perfectly tailored pinstriped navy suit. He resembled Robert Mitchum, with salt and pepper hair, a strong jaw and steely blue eyes. He brought me a beautiful bouquet of spring flowers; I was touched. I began our conversation saying, "Look, I don't know how lucrative the company is. Sometimes, there's lots of money in the business account and sometimes there is not. I told him about the government contracts I was familiar with. I knew several contracts Steve worked with steadily. I had seen checks for $90,000 made out to Latitude from several of these companies. One was with a company called Dynamax and another I recalled was Pharmscience. Before Steve fell ill, he would call me from work and say, "Hey babe, I need you to be home today and on the lookout for some checks coming by FedEx." He would tell me to call him as soon as the checks arrived and let him know the exact amount of each. I always obliged my husband because I knew this was very important to him. I remember at the funeral the CEO and owner of Dynamax was present. He walked over to me and introduced himself as Fred Pierce, president of Dynamax. The gentleman continued and said to me, "We'll keep doing business with Latitude, I promise you." I shook my head with gratitude and replied, "Great, sounds good to me." I knew that the contract was still good for another three years because Steve had signed a five-year contract two years prior to his death.

The same thing happened with Pharmscience. There would be checks for $30,000 delivered to our front door. I told Mitch about these companies. I told the man everything I knew about Latitude. Mitch seemed kind, gracious and forthcoming. I thought I was a pretty good judge of character. During our conversation, Mitch mentioned his background in the military and geospatial contracts. He said he believed the company was in trouble and needed help desperately. I agreed with him one hundred percent. I sold Mitch the company for a mere $5,000.00. I wanted out. I thought in the end, Latitude was going to drain my money dry. At the time, I believed it was the best decision I could possibly make, given the circumstances. In our pending contract, Mitch agreed to pay me five percent each year of the unaudited profits, going into effect at the end of that first fiscal year.

I spoke to an attorney before I officially sold or signed anything. The attorney asked me lots of questions I did not have the answers to. Questions like, "Well, are you selling the assets, or are you selling the shares?" I replied, "I don't know. I don't know anything. What's an asset? What's a share?" I honestly didn't know. I'm a piano teacher and trainer. How could I possibly know what the heck I was selling? I thought I was selling the name, the employees, the contracts and ultimately the business. I felt good about selling this company. It was a huge relief for me just thinking it would be off my shoulders and placed on someone else's more competent shoulders. We set a date to meet for the signing and official sale of the company. Mitch Halliday, myself, Don Allston, Dick Richards and Gene Dickinson, (Steve's accountant) who also worked for Latitude, were present at my kitchen table one week after my initial meeting with Mitch. I was so excited to finally exhale about this matter and feel comfortable the company would be in competent hands. Mitch sat at the head of the table and introduced himself politely to the other gentlemen present. Don was squirming in his seat and appeared very uncomfortable with the situation. Dick and Gene seemed indifferent about the whole meeting. I remember feeling happy and proud of myself for finding someone qualified to take over ownership of the company.

Suddenly, Don stood up from the table and said, "Kate, I need to speak with you privately, now!" I looked at him with a quizzical expression and said, "Of course, let's go into the other room." Don immediately started yelling that this was ridiculous. He told me not to sell the company and that he would help me run it moving forward. I listened with shock and disbelief to his tantrum and replied softly, "I need to do this for me. I need time to grieve my husband, and I can't do that if I'm worrying about his company 24/7." Don was not happy with my comment, and his true colors came shining through that instant. He got right up close to my face with his and said tauntingly, "Is it for the money? Are you selling Latitude for the money?" I broke down and cried, saying over and over again, "No, this is about my sanity. I can't even walk into the building because I don't have a clearance! How in the name of heaven could I run this company? I am a piano teacher and a trainer, for goodness sake. I can't even read a map, let alone create one! I'm selling Latitude, and that's final!" I proceeded to walk away and slam the door behind me.

I signed the contract, and so did Mitch. The deal was done.

The following morning, Mitch and I ventured to the bank to switch names on the business account. Upon entering the bank, an outspoken woman named KiKi came running up to me with arms open wide and a broad smile. She said, "I'm so sorry for your loss, kiddo." I replied shakily, "Yes, thank you so much." After a hug that seemed to last an eternity, she let go of me and looked at Mitch and said, "Now, how can I be of service to you today?" We sat down at her desk and signed some papers, and the name was switched.

I was relieved that the company was no longer mine. One thing down, and a million to go! Another daunting task I had to tackle was dealing with the Social Security office. I had to call Social Security because Jack and I were entitled to Steve's money each month. I was told the payments would start in June. I would receive a larger check for the months of April and May combined. The woman I met with was very cordial. She asked me a bunch of questions; I provided the death certificate and was out of there in twenty minutes. I was very relieved to know I would receive a social security check monthly, no matter what.

Meanwhile, Don Allston had more surprises for me. When he cleaned out Steve's desk, it was like opening

Pandora's Box. Don came to me and said, "Look, there are a few things I've uncovered, and you need to be informed. He continued to tell me that Steve had many credit cards still open with heavy balances owed. I looked at Don with shock and disbelief and said, "That's impossible. We weren't using credit cards. There were only two, a Visa, and a Master Card. He replied, "No. I'm sorry, that's simply not true." I sat there shaking my head thinking, "What the heck was my husband doing?" I was now responsible for paying off every single credit card Steve owned. Although they were not in my name, I was the estate of Steve Williams and ultimately responsible. There were all kinds of credit cards; silver, elite, high status ones with a $50,000-dollar limit, a $75,000-dollar limit, a $25,000-dollar limit, and every card was maxed out. I went home and called each credit card company one by one. I told them who I was and what happened and paid them off, every single one of them. The amount totaled over $250,000.00. It was a huge chunk of money, but I had no choice.

Steve drove a black Audi when he was alive. I explained to Hunter, "I've got to sell this car." I looked up the Kelly Blue Book value and discovered I could sell it for $3,500.00 in good condition. The car was a year 2000 and Steve kept it immaculate. Hunter said, "I'll buy it." How much do you want?" I said, "$3,500." He wrote me a check, and the car was his. Hunter told me he was looking for a car rather than driving his truck everywhere.

Happy Birthday

I thought it was a win/win situation. I was glad the car would be with someone who would take care of it and appreciate its value.

At the same time, I found out about my car, a 2004 cream-colored Lexus. When Steve bought it, he told me he paid cash for the price of the car. His exact words were, "Yeah, babe, it's paid off." I loved the car and was grateful Steve was willing to let go of his sports car and drive the Audi when his symptoms worsened. His sports car was stick shift and with his lack of movement and failing reflexes, driving a TT was out of the question. I assumed Steve was telling me the truth when he said he paid cash for my Lexus. When Don approached me with a small pamphlet resembling a car note, I knew Steve lied. He didn't pay cash for the entire amount; he financed the car. Don found the car payment vouchers in Steve's desk.

I was starting to panic. Since Steve died, I had discovered empty bank accounts, many outstanding credit cards, a car note he lied about, and I was dealing with some guy threatening me because Steve owed him a bunch of money. I had received several letters and two phone calls from some weird company saying Steve owed $40,000 for money he borrowed. I had no idea if this was a scam or if my late husband had actually borrowed money from a loan shark, paying 50% interest on the loan. I had no sense of security. One day, I answered my phone, and a man's voice said very sternly, "Is this Mrs. Williams?" I replied shakily, "Yes, who is this?" He continued to tell me that I better pay, or things would not be good for Jack and me. My heart was racing, and I was terrified. I could not distinguish between what was real and what was a lie. The man I married and had a child with had done things I could never imagine him doing. My whole sense of reality was twisted. Not only had he lied to me to my face, but now I had to listen to a strange man threatening me and my little boy! Why would Steve do this to me? How could he leave me in such a vulnerable position? Why was he dealing with such despicable people? I remember thinking, "He made good money, we lived within our means, and he told me we were fine financially." I could not stop the constant barrage of questions swimming in my head. God help me.

CHAPTER 6

Fair-Weather Friends

My hands were shaking, and I had a sick, nauseating feeling in my stomach as I read the hand written letter from Martin (my son-in-law). Martin was an odd bird. He stood about 5'11" with a shaved head, sloped shoulders and thick, black rimmed glasses that constantly slipped down the bridge of his nose causing him to push them up every five minutes, like a nervous tick. He insisted on wearing jeans approximately two sizes too small for his body, (apparently the "hipster" style is all the rage with young people). I wondered how his privates could stand the ridiculously tight jeans he wore daily.

Needless to say, he was quite the character. In June, only two months after Steve's death, I received a letter from Martin. His letter read like a high school drop-out's attempt at sounding intelligent. I knew Martin had dropped out of college a few years back and had very little formal education. He had earned his GED while working in a coffee shop supporting himself. He had told me his birth mother died and his step mother was a raging alcoholic who kicked him out of the house at age seventeen. I gave him credit for finding a job, an apartment and means to support himself at such a young age. He was definitely a mover and a shaker. Anyway, in his hand-written letter, he asked for many small items that were given to me by Steve and his mother, Doris. Family heirlooms, engagement gifts and sentimental woodwork made by Steve's dad. These items were mine and Steve's together. I cherished them. There were a few little chairs that Steve's father had made; one was for Jack. We had pictures taken of Jack in that chair wearing his grandfather's cowboy hat. Those items meant a lot to Jack because we told him they belonged to his "Grandpa." I put the little chair and cowboy hat in his room, and Jack adored both.

Samantha requested many sentimental items. She asked for Steve's vintage album collection. Steve had a remarkable record collection of Pink Floyd, David Bowie and the Rolling Stones. Steve loved the classics. He had special albums that were unseen because he was a collector. He had the frames imported from Germany. Together, we framed the albums and hung them in our family room. Every time I looked at those album covers, I thought of Steve and smiled. Samantha also had the nerve to ask for my furniture. These pieces had been in our home for seven years. When Steve and I combined our stuff, it was a crazy collection of modern meets traditional. I believe the word is "eclectic."

It seemed Samantha wanted everything! I was completely flabbergasted by her brazen requests only weeks after Steve's death. Her list included a certain antique dresser that was actually in our bedroom, the rocking chair I rocked Jack in when he was a baby, a wedding vase given to me by Doris (which Steve and I cherished), and Steve's entire vintage record collection! Many of these items held huge sentimental value. I was shocked that she was shamelessly asking for these items and expecting me to just provide them without hesitation. I didn't even have an address for her at the time. Steve's Memorial Service was the last time I laid eyes on Samantha or Martin.

Jack's birthday, Easter and Mother's Day all had passed by this time, and we had heard nothing from Samantha or Martin. I was shocked by them asking for all these items in this handwritten letter. I texted Martin and said, "I'm really not ready to do all of this right now; however, I can give you Loren's table that was promised to Samantha. Steve and I were storing a beautiful, hand-made (by Steve's dad) kitchen table. It had been her grandfather's and was promised to Samantha by Steve. We were storing it in our garage. I said, "I can get the table together, and I'll add the stereo with antique speakers." I actually gave them an old-fashioned stereo Steve had cherished with huge speakers that sounded amazing. I packed it all up and prepared to ship it to Martin and Samantha. Martin texted me their new address, and Hunter graciously offered to drive the items right to their doorstep.

Steve loved antiques. He maintained the same old

125

furniture for over twenty years. My late husband was completely content with the same stuff forever. My furniture was more modern and contemporary, so we combined our styles and made it work. Samantha was familiar with what was in our home because when Steve was well, she came over frequently. However, when Steve fell ill, we never saw her or Martin, no matter how much I begged.

Martin said it would mean a lot to Samantha to have these items. The truth is, they were my things. They were mine and Steve's together. One of the pieces they asked for was a wedding vase that had been in Steve's family for many years. Steve's mother, Doris, gave it to me as a "welcome to our family." I couldn't believe Samantha had the audacity to demand she acquire this particular vase.

After Hunter graciously put Samantha's table in his truck and delivered it to their home, Martin texted me that one of the legs was broken. The table needed to be fixed before we packed it up. I packed it carefully and as best I could. Samantha knew it needed to be fixed. Steve had explained to her that the leg was loose and needed a new screw to tighten it properly. This information was not unknown to her. Steve's father was a master carpenter and had a passion for repurposing old furniture. The table was beautiful and just needed a little tender loving care. It seemed to me Martin and Samantha were blaming me for the broken, wooden leg on the table. Hunter was kind enough to deliver the table to their front door. There was no gratitude or appreciation for my efforts. They simply complained about the table leg and blamed me.

Another issue surrounded by drama concerned the life insurance policies Steve carried. Steve had several life insurance policies naming me as the sole beneficiary on all of them except one. I assumed I was the beneficiary on every policy Steve held. After calling all the appropriate phone numbers for this particular policy, I discovered I was not. The woman I spoke to on the other end of the phone could not legally tell me who the beneficiary was. I just assumed if it wasn't me, it must be Samantha. Maybe Steve left her something, after all? Unfortunately, before knowing who the benefactor was, I told Martin and Samantha the policy must be for them. I forwarded all the contact information on the policy to Martin. I felt good that Steve left them some money. I never gave that policy a second thought. Days later, Martin called me and said, "Kate, Samantha is not the beneficiary, and we have no idea who was named." I was in shock. I fumbled with my words and told him I too had no idea who it could be. From Martin's snippy response, I believe he thought I was lying. There was absolutely nothing I could do about this situation. I was as flabbergasted and dumbfounded as Martin and Samantha. I asked my attorney if there was any way to find out who the beneficiary was. Robert told me I would know shortly and meanwhile, don't lose sleep over the matter.

I was following the advice of my boss at the gym,

ALMOST SHATTERED

Mike, of simply inhaling then exhaling and repeating this one day at a time. The days seemed to creep by, and I had constant companions of anxiety and tension. I remember feeling a palpable, impending sense of doom. I could not shake this feeling, no matter how hard I tried. Then, it happened. My worst nightmare was staring me in the face. It was a sunny, unusually warm day in June, and I walked outside to grab the mail. There were several bills and sympathy cards from friends, and I spotted the handwritten letter with the return address of Martin and Samantha. I was curious but not alarmed. I tore open the letter and as I began to read the almost illegible hand-written letter, my heart nearly stopped. Sweat began to trickle down my brow and my heart-rate skyrocketed along with my blood pressure. I couldn't see, I was dizzy. I couldn't hear anyone because something cracked inside my brain blocking out all sound except the banging of stone with a hammer between my ears. The words on the page in front of me demanded $170,000.00. Martin continued to say this amount of money should be easy for me to part with, and I owed it to both him and his wife. He also intimated that I needed to give them this money so life would remain tolerable for my son and me. However, if I chose to decline their request, my life would change dramatically for the worse. Martin continued in his letter to tell me he and Samantha were entitled to this money because it was Samantha's birthright (or some crazy, nonsensical logic). He said he was thrilled I found someone so soon after Steve's death. He sarcastically stated he hoped things worked out for me and my new beau. He laid the final blow when he stated he and Samantha could not be in relationship with me or Jack. Martin claimed it would be just "too hard" for Samantha to see us. My God!! What on earth did Jack have to do with any of this? He was just a five-year-old, innocent little boy who lost his father tragically. Jack adored his "Sissy" (Samantha) and Uncle Martin. He jumped for joy any time they came to the house. I was absolutely sick. I felt the vomit in the back of my throat form as I finished reading their letter. After telling me he could no longer be in relationship with Jack or me, he threatened litigation if I did not pay the amount they were asking for promptly. I held the letter in my trembling hands, fell to my knees and cried like I've never cried before.

Martin and Samantha were terribly misinformed about my financial status. It appeared they believed I was "loaded." This could not be further from the truth. I had a few life insurance policies come to fruition, no job to speak of, an extremely high mortgage, and thousands upon thousands of dollars to pay for Steve's credit card debt! They were completely misinformed. Although they felt justified asking for $170,000, these two upstarts had no business receiving any money Steve left for Jack and me. They actually believed I was set for life! This naïve and very desperate couple were attempting to blackmail me. It was as evident to me as the back of my hand. After some of the shock wore off, I called my attorney, Robert Banks, and told him about the blackmail letter. He suggested I come in and meet with him to discuss this matter. He told me to calm down and stop stressing about the situation. That felt like he was telling the wind to stop blowing!

Martin was brazen enough to tell me that Steve met secretly with Samantha every week for lunch. He continued to explain that Samantha cried every time she left our home after a visit. Martin also claimed that Steve promised him, about a year back, that he would "take care" of him and Samantha. When he mentioned this, my heart began to pound inside my chest like a beating drum. I could not imagine Steve ever meeting with his daughter and not telling me. I would have been delighted for both of them if they were meeting for lunch! All I wanted was for Samantha to spend as much time with her father as possible before it was too late. I was beginning to believe my late husband did many things in secret. The reality was that he lied about money, cars, credit cards and his family. Who on earth did I marry? Did I even really know this man?? I could not escape the multitude of questions pounding in my brain.

Martin was strange. He stood about 6 ft. tall with an average-size frame. He shaved his head and wore thick black glasses to correct his wandering, left eye. Martin came into our lives a few years back and was still relatively new to the family. He was shameless in his requests for money, furniture, family heirlooms, and so on. One thought kept coming back to me during this time, "Who, in the name of heaven, does this guy think he is?" He is not even a blood relative. He is a grown man who needs to get a job to support his wife and coming child. Samantha had found out she was pregnant right before Steve died. They both told us one night at dinner that she was having baby. I was overjoyed! I remember feeling so excited for them. I was also thrilled that I would be a grandmother! Knowing Martin was jobless, newly married and a first time, expectant father, no wonder he was blackmailing me for money; he was desperate.

My attorney, Robert Banks, advised me that no response was the best response to the ridiculous letter from Martin. Robert also said that until there is an attorney made evident, maintain peace of mind regarding this matter. I felt good about him saying these things to me with such sincerity. I trusted Robert with my life.

There are two facts about Steve that are absolutely true. One, he never, ever did anything he didn't want to do. Two, he was brilliant. Steve chose to leave Samantha a small amount of money in a CD at the Credit Union. Martin was her covering now because they were married. Steve never wanted to undermine Martin's authority as a husband. In Steve's will he specifically stated, "There is no provision for my daughter, Samantha." It doesn't get much clearer than that! She and Martin chose not to visit us when Steve was ill. They never came around for dinner, a chat or even to see Jack. It crushed Steve; it was written all over his face. He loved his daughter deeply. He went to every soccer game, dance, awards dinner and more! Anything that girl was involved in, Steve was present, up close and personal. He even coached her soccer team for two years. Steve was an excellent dad in every sense of the word. It was hard for him to express just how much pain Samantha caused him when he fell ill. Steve felt stained, marked, like damaged goods as a dad. The lack of Samantha's presence in his life confirmed those feelings every day.

.When I received the second letter, I noticed it was from a law firm. I thought, "Here we go! They want everything I have. I'm going to have to fight for security for the rest of my life!" I opened the letter quickly rather than slowly. I thought it might be less painful (like ripping a band aid off fast). This letter was not as informal as the previous one from Martin. It was written by some paralegal and signed by Daniel Deveroux, Esq., and it demanded money–lots of it. Worse yet, the attorney tried to support his demand for cash by claiming that I had been abusive to Steve. His letter read, "Mrs. Williams was known to be verbally and emotionally abusive to her husband. She also withheld food from Mr. Williams to keep him weak and malnourished." My stomach began to churn, and the room was spinning. I felt as if I would faint at any moment as I continued to read. The second paragraph stated, "Mrs. Williams was demanding and selfish. She coerced her husband into signing his will." It went on, "After all, the will was all Kate's idea. According to Samantha, Steve Williams' daughter, Kate used her power of influence and the threat of divorce any time she wanted something from Steve." I stood there in my kitchen, and I realized my heart was racing, my blood pressure shot through the roof and my face felt hot, uncomfortably hot. I could not find my speech to talk. My tongue felt like it weighed one hundred pounds every time I tried to utter one word. Sweat gathered on my upper lip and under my arms and down my back. I had the distinct urge to run. I wanted to grab Jack, throw some things in a bag and get gone. How in the world and why in the world would these two young people, whom I loved dearly, hurt me this way?? Did they not know lying (known as perjury) is punishable by imprisonment? I've read that the human survival instincts when threatened are fight, flight or freeze. I was definitely in "flight" mode. I thought to myself, "Why not? I have enough money to live for a while somewhere new. I could start over, reinvent myself. I could change my look entirely!" This pervasive thought would not leave my mind. I was living in my fantasized future, not the real present.

The one thing I could hold on to, or so I thought at the time, was my financial status. I received many life insurance policies, had a good amount in savings and received Steve's social security death benefit monthly (it was a good chunk of change). Thinking about the money made me feel better. When you have a lot of money, you have power. The quote, "Money talks," is absolutely valid. Money speaks its own language. Those who have never had a lot, never learn to speak the, "I have tons of money" language. I was learning to speak this new lingo for the first time in my life. I felt safe, secure and protected because I knew no matter what life threw at me, I could cover it financially. When my thoughts raced to Samantha and Martin attempting to steal the only thing (at the time) that made me feel safe, I was swallowed by panic. I literally lived inside sheer, unadulterated panic. Why would they want to jeopardize little Jack's future? How could they hurt this innocent, little boy they claimed to love so dearly? None of this was making sense to me at the time. Although my funds appeared ample, Steve's incurred debt was staggering! He had over twenty outstanding credit cards that I had to pay off. It appeared no one wanted to address any of these facts, except for me.

I also had the multitude of medical bills from Steve's illness to contend with. The medical bills were outrageous. I paid every single one as they came in, and they just kept coming. I wondered if they would ever stop. There were bills for MRIs, X-rays, blood draws, specialized testing, consultations and many urinalyses. The total for Steve's medical debt was well over $50,000.00. I paid every dime. I didn't know what else to do! Ultimately, the "estate" of Steve Williams was responsible for these bills. Guess who was the "estate" of Steve Williams, ME!!

Fair-Weather Friends

I received an interesting call from Steve's insurance lady, Babs (short for Barbara, but she insisted on Babs) Goldberg. This lady was hilarious. I really liked her from the moment we met. Babs was your typical New York, Jewish lady. She was loud and animated in her speech. Her hair was huge, and she was twenty pounds overweight in her chest! Her clothes were always colorful and bedazzled. Babs was "walking bling!" Although her outward appearance was brazen and shocking, she had a huge heart. Babs was empathic and kind to me. Babs had lost her husband just two years prior to Steve passing. She understood the utter shock and total devastation of losing a spouse. Babs became my ally. She called regularly, told me who to contact at Social Security, who to call for different policies and to simply enjoy my money! She said to me in her heavy Brooklyn accent, "Kate, enjoy your money, enjoy your money." She continued, "Screw them." That's how she would talk. "Screw those greedy bastards," that's Babs in a nutshell! She said, "Enjoy your money, sweetheart. You earned it. You deserve it. Spouses take care of spouses." Babs said something I'll never forget. After I told her what Steve's daughter was doing, she said, "Who?" I explained, "You know his only daughter, 26 years old, married...ring a bell?" She cleared her throat and dispassionately stated, "Steve Williams spoke of only one child and one family. That was you and Jack. I had no idea he had another child or an ex-wife for that matter!"

I was stunned. I felt happy but stunned. "Wow, only one family... interesting," I pondered.

The constant, annoying feeling of fear was always with me, like my shadow. I've heard it said many times, "Desperate people do desperate things." Martin was without a job; his wife was pregnant and he was newly married. Samantha certainly didn't contribute financially. She told me more than once over the years that her goal, after graduating college, was to be a wife and a mother. I never understood this mindset. I was raised to have a career and be independent. My dad would always say to me, "Ish (my nickname), you're not going to college to get your 'MRS' Degree!" So, I thought, you go to college, work, see the world and then settle down.

I never stopped praying. I prayed morning, noon and night about this whole crazy situation with Samantha and Martin. The Lord was putting kindness, forgiveness and compassion on my heart. I pictured all of us reuniting and hugging and kissing and being very close. I decided to call Martin. I thought, "We are all just people trying to deal with this terrible loss." I thought if I reached out with a sincere and honest heart, the results would be amazing! No one else in my circle believed this was a good idea. My mother told me numerous times to leave Colorado and live in Texas near her and Drew. Hunter wanted to eliminate the problem by having one of his buddies pay Martin a little visit! I told Hunter emphatically, "NO! We are never going to be those people who harm others in any way!" I continued to explain to Hunter that God's punishment is one hundred-fold worse than anything man can do! I explained to Hunter emphatically, "Martin and Samantha are both Christians. I'm a Christian. The power of prayer can change anything." I continued, "Love is the only force that can turn an enemy into a friend. I'm going to be naked in front of them with my feelings. I'm going to be raw and tell them how I feel." I called Martin and I said, "Hey Martin, it's Kate. Could we talk for minute?" He replied casually, "Yeah, sure." He said, "Hey, Kate," as if nothing was going on and everything was normal. I spoke eagerly, "Look, I love you guys. I don't know what's going on with these letters of yours and (I hesitated nervously), I'm a little confused, but I'd like for us to meet sometime soon. I'd very much like to give you a gift." I kept talking because I assumed Martin was listening intently, "I want to give you guys $10,000 to help with the birth of the baby. You'll be able to buy the things you need. Babies need lots of stuff." I laughed a bit nervously and added, "I'd love for you both to come over and spend time with little Jack; he misses you a lot. Let's really try." I thought to myself, "Wow, I did it! I was authentic and brutally honest with him." I was completely real. Before Martin could respond to my suggestion, I said choking back tears, "I'm hurting and I'm scared. I don't know what's happening from one day to the next, and I think we could all get through this a lot easier if we stuck together." He said, "Okay, how about Sunday?

ALMOST SHATTERED

We'll come Sunday." I said with a huge smile on my face, "That would be great!" and I hung up the phone. I was so excited for that Sunday. I thought that I had solved the problem. I'm going to give them a gift. Everything's going to be great. We're going to take it step by step and one day at a time.

After my conversation with Martin, the very next day, he sent me a text that read, "Your offer is a slap in the face. We don't want anything from you. We will take care of our child alone, by ourselves, and we cannot be in relationship with you or Jack at this time." Oh my God, why? I kept reading and rereading his hateful and bitter words over and over. I must have stood there for twenty minutes, not moving, just reading. I asked myself two questions, "What just happened, and why on earth did Martin's attitude change so suddenly?"

The next few days brought a multitude of feelings and emotions. I felt anger, extreme sadness, fear, loneliness and abandonment. My anger felt like a fire that started in my brain and coursed throughout my entire being. There was only one place to vent this rage. The rage and I went to the gym every day! I pounded on the punching bag, ran for miles on the track and lifted the heaviest weights I could find! Nothing matches the feeling of lifting 195lbs. when you only weigh 115lbs. I rode that high for days! Along with the anger came extreme hurt. I was truly devastated by their words and actions. I couldn't stop thinking about what the future held.

Fair-Weather Friends

Meanwhile, I kept trying to live one moment at a time. "Do the next right thing, Kate, just do the next right thing," is what I kept telling myself over and over. The third letter arrived. In this particular letter, the attorney was requesting a copy of Steve's will. He lowered the monetary amount to $150,000 and threatened if I didn't pay the money and have a copy of Steve's will promptly on his desk, litigation was imminent. I sat down, hung my head between my legs and sobbed. Were they actually planning on taking me to court? I pictured myself on the stand, being accused of these horrible things! What was happening? I was terrified. The letter also explained that I had a certain amount of time to respond with my answer or court was inevitable. I stopped wallowing in my self-pity and fear and called Robert Banks. Robert was a seasoned attorney, approximately mid-forties, with a gentle smile that I always found comforting. He wasn't terribly attractive, but his gentle manner and kind expression were endearing. Robert didn't judge me. He listened intently and never responded very quickly to my anxious questions. He always took his time, and every word he spoke was with intention. His ever-present state of calm was contagious. When Robert answered the phone, I breathlessly explained my situation. I explained to Robert (with much emotion) my confusion and fear about Martin and Samantha's requests. I rattled on about how they never helped when Steve was sick. I told him about the many times I begged them to come over for dinner or coffee or simply to visit. And that their answer was always, "We would love to, but we're both very busy." Robert continued to listen to my tale of woe and misery and politely suggested I bring him the will and the letters received from Martin and the attorney, Mr. Deveroux, Esq.

The following day I was in Robert's office with both the will and the letters. Robert calmly sat down, read all four items and stated, "This is absurd and cruel. I'm so sorry, Kate. These two kids are essentially trying to extort money and blackmail you, both of which are very much against the law." He added, "This is ridiculous." I was immediately relieved by his assessment. However, I still had questions. I asked, "Can they force me pay them this money? Will they ask for more? What else do you think they want?" Robert looked at me intently and said," They can ask for the moon; it doesn't mean they'll ever get it."

After I had let out a huge sigh of relief, Robert explained that life insurance money does not pass through the will. He continued to explain, "No one can touch that money Steve intended for you and Jack. The will is public knowledge. Anyone can go to the courthouse and request a copy of any will at any time. Mr. Deveroux is simply bullying you, Kate. He is using intimidation tactics and threats to get you to write a check. Don't do it." Although I trusted Robert implicitly and he was absolutely one hundred percent correct, I couldn't shake the uneasiness and anxiety sticking to me like crazy glue.

Fair-Weather Friends

I remember one afternoon, I found myself alone in my gigantic house. The sunlight came pouring in through the large windows on the cathedral ceiling. I felt a sense of nostalgia and comfort. I recalled the past seven years of my life and all the memories I had with Samantha. I was her "go-to" parent. She always called me first. If she was in trouble, scared, happy, excited or uncertain, she called me before Steve and before her birth mother. I felt honored she considered me a confidant. I held everything she told me in trust. I gave her the best advice I could offer. One particular phone call came from the University she was attending. It was a member of their medical staff. I answered the phone and the voice on the other end said sternly, "We have Samantha Williams in our office, and we need to speak with a legal guardian immediately." I was instantly alarmed and answered," What's wrong? Is Samantha ok? Is she in trouble? An accident?" The stern voice softened slightly and replied, "No, nothing like that. Your daughter is having suicidal ideations. She is here with us, so she will remain safe. Legally I have to bring her for a psychological evaluation and keep her for a minimum of 72 hours. You can come visit her at St. Mary's Hospital in the behavioral unit. St. Mary's has an excellent Mental Health Department." I was so shaken by this news, I stuttered and said, "Uh, of course, we will head there shortly and thank you." I remember explaining the situation to Steve, and he cried. Steve rarely cried. We packed up baby Jack and headed to Topeka, Kansas, eight hours away. Years later, Samantha called me in a state of hysteria. Through her sobs she said her boyfriend had ended things. He broke up with her because he wasn't ready to be in a committed relationship (after three years of dating her). I told her I was very sorry and that she needed to breathe and that her dad and I were coming to get her immediately. When Samantha was preparing for her wedding, she nervously asked me to sing at their ceremony. Not only did she ask me to sing, but she requested I compose a song for her and Martin to walk down the aisle. I was honored by her request, and I told her I absolutely would do both. I answered, "I'll write the song and sing and play it at your wedding ceremony, no problem!"

Along with the fond memories came some ugly ones. Samantha had this interesting way of changing the pitch of her voice to that of a little girl instead of the grown woman she was. One day I heard her talking to Steve in that silly, child-like tone. I called her on it. I said, "Stop. Stop talking like that. Why are you talking like that? Where is your real voice? You're a grown woman, talk like one." She looked at me with daggers in her eyes! Boy, was she mad. She acted like she had no idea what I was talking about. She actually said," What do you mean?" I calmly explained that her voice changes dramatically when she asks her dad for money, a credit card or help of some sort. I told her it's important to have a voice as a woman, human and as an adult. The little girl whimper makes you appear naïve, ignorant and silly. I further explained, as a college graduate and 22-year-old intelligent woman, she needed to find her voice and utilize it. I don't think Samantha ever forgave me for that day!

To make things worse, the loan shark contacted me daily. The letters were coming directly to the house. It looked like an ordinary letter addressed to Latitude, Inc., but it came to my house, not to the PO Box business address. I opened the letter, and it read, "Dear Mrs. Williams, you owe us $40,000.00. We need you to pay immediately. You must pay this debt. I thought, "Oh no, if Steve himself personally took out the money or borrowed the money, do I owe it back? Does the estate of Steve Williams owe this money back to these people?" I was scared! I put it aside. There was just too much drama and chaos in my life, so I decided to simply put it aside. A couple of weeks later, I received a phone call, and a gentleman's voice gruffly said, "Is this Kate Williams?" I said, "Who's calling?" His name was Paul or something like that. "This is Paul, blah blah blah." I asked, "What do you want?" He replied, "We want what's owed to us." I stammered, "I don't even know what you're talking about." He said, "Your husband owes us $40,000." He continued firmly, "We need to get the money, one way or another." I'm thinking, "Oh, my God, what the heck is that supposed to mean?" I asked frantically, "Are you threatening me? Is this a threat?" He said, "Consider it whatever you want, but we will get our money," and hung up. My heart was racing, adrenaline pumping hard and fast and my head hurt. My thoughts were scrambled, and I painted morbid scenarios in my mind like, "Oh my God, I'm going to be killed, or kidnapped or worse… they'll go for Jack! God help me!

I called Robert Banks. I screeched, "Robert, what the heck is this? Do I have to leave the country? What should I do? He said, "Calm down. Bring me the letter. Let's revisit what the guy said. Let's go over it." He said, "Look, they're just trying to bully you, trying to threaten you. Don't do anything. When in doubt, do nothing." I said, "Yeah, but they know where I live. They have my address."

I made sure the alarm worked. I tightened up the locks, secured everything. This made me feel a little better. Also, I had Hunter, and Hunter is a very intimidating person. He's sleeved in ink, muscles bulging everywhere and maintains a threatening persona. Hunter has a presence that intimidates. I was so anxious and frightened because the guy said, "We're going to get our money, one way or another." Those words kept repeating in my mind over and over. Hunter said, "You're not giving those people anything. You're not giving anybody anything." He said, "Kate, you can't see the forest through the trees because of your emotional state, but I can! Both of them, Samantha and Martin, and whoever this guy is, this loan shark, they are both trying to bully you into writing a check." He was right; that's exactly what they were doing.

Fair-Weather Friends

I made the decision to simply stand. Stand in truth with my armor on, and let the Lord do the rest!

My relationships with those I thought were my best friends suffered greatly during this time. Steve and I had been close friends with Sue and Dick for years. I thought they were my best friends. Dick worked for Steve, and Sue and I got along extremely well. We went to dinner with this couple almost every weekend. We drank together, shopped together and laughed a lot together! I wanted Dick and Sue to meet Hunter and like him and be happy for me. We planned to go to dinner, the four of us, one evening. I got the distinct impression that they both did not like Hunter. They missed Steve. They never even gave Hunter a chance. At dinner, Dick asked the craziest questions of Hunter, like he was my dad or something! He asked, "What are your feelings here? What are your intentions with Kate?" Hunter replied, "I love Kate, and it's none of your business." That didn't go over so well with either Dick or Sue. Hunter also told both of them that he was committed to me in every sense of the word and wanted to marry me. We finished dinner with small talk and went our separate ways. The evening was extremely strained and awkward. During the following weeks, I didn't hear from Sue once. I was so troubled by their reaction to Hunter and me. I asked myself a million times, "Don't they want me to be happy? Aren't they excited for me?"

Finally, on week three after our dinner date together,

Dick called. He sounded odd and hesitant on the phone. I inquired, genuinely concerned, and asked, "What's wrong, buddy? Are you ok? How can I help?" He cleared his throat abruptly and said, "Kate, I need a favor. We have struggled over the past six months, just trying to make ends meet. Could you give me some money to help pay our taxes?" I replied instantly, "Of course! Whatever you need, you got it!" Dick asked me for $5,000.00. I handed him a check that afternoon. I never saw Dick or Sue again.

CHAPTER 7

Find a Way

O ne night in the middle of all this, I was watching "Dancing with the Stars." Steve and I loved that show, and it meant a lot to me to keep watching it. Diana Nyad was a contestant on the show that season. She was a woman in her 60's who swam from Cuba to Florida in unprotected waters. It took her seven tries, but she finally succeeded. No one had ever done it before, nobody. She was just an ordinary woman. An ordinary woman who had a passion for swimming and loved a challenge!

She had made it through the first few rounds of "Dancing with the Stars," so the show was focusing on her more. The host of the show asked, "Well, how were you able to achieve your swimming victory?" She said something that I'll never forget as long as I live. She said, "I thought to myself, I'm going to find a way. I must find a way." She continued, "And that's what I told myself every day. Find a way."

I was so struck by that, by her tenacity and her not giving up attitude, and that she didn't surrender. She thought, "I'm going to do this. I can do this. I can do it.

ALMOST SHATTERED

If it takes me ten tries, or if it takes me twenty tries, I'm going to do it." I remember thinking, "Oh, my gosh!" She talked about the jellyfish that stung her and the sharks in the water. She had a team beside her, helping her, but there was no safety net. She talked about the sunburn and the dehydration and everything she went through. I thought, "Holy cow. If she can make it through that ordeal, I can certainly handle my situation. I don't have jellyfish attacking me and there's no threat of sharks (other than a loan shark)."

That was a big revelation for me. I thought, "This is it! Things are changing. I'm going to buck up. I need to take care of myself, put down the alcohol, get back to the gym, and start feeding my body the right food. It was like the Rocky theme was playing in the background. That's how I felt. It was one of those moments when for that short period of time, everything appeared crystal clear.

I started by saying the words out loud. I spoke the words boldly with confidence, "I'm going to find a way. I'm going to find a way to do this. I will get through this." I kept thinking, "I'm not going to cave. I'm not going to give in to them; just because they want something from me, doesn't mean I have to give it to them."

I remember that I was sitting in my favorite spot on our sofa where Steve and I used to sit, and tears were streaming down my face. I was crying, but tears of joy. I knew then that it was going to be okay. Somehow, some way, I was going to power through this, and I was going to be victorious. I was going to find a way through it, every single day.

Diana Nyad had to find a way through every obstacle each day that it took her to get to Florida by swimming. She had the jellyfish attack one day, starvation on another day, leg cramps another day, and the entire time sharks were circling; her team frantically trying to bat them away. Seriously, there were sharks everywhere! She had to find a way each day to get through that nightmare.

I started thinking about things in terms of one day at a time. It's the only way I could look at my life in order to survive and cope. Some people get drunk when there is a crisis or turn to drugs. Others might jump off a building or surrender and give people what they want without a fight. I vowed whatever each new day brings, I will handle it like a champion with grace and candor. In that moment, I knew exactly what it was going to take; tenacity and resolve. It was time for me to put my big girl panties on and get to work.

The rest of 2014 brought its own challenges, like the ones I'd been experiencing since Steve died. I had been getting letters, maybe one a week, from the loan sharks, demanding their money. My attorney believed they were shady in some way and didn't want to draw attention to themselves. He again said, "Do not lose sleep over this." Soon after I had my revelation about Diana Nyad, I got another call from them, saying basically the same things, "We want our money, we'll get it one way or another.

We've been patient, we've been waiting," blah, blah, blah. I hung up. I didn't even listen. I just hung up.

I had grown closer to Pastor Angelo at the time of Steve's death and memorial service. I had attended his church for nearly seven years, taught Sunday school and played on the worship team. I was certainly involved. After reconnecting with him on a more personal level at the memorial service, I thought I'd have a friend for life, a support person. He even went so far as to tell me, "If you don't get any money, I'll help you."

I was having anxiety one day, badly; I couldn't eat, couldn't sleep, and I was starting to get what I thought was some sort of cold or flu. I had no idea what was happening to me physically! So, I called Pastor Angelo. I called him out of the blue because he said, "Call me anytime." I was standing in my kitchen; I'll never forget it, Liz was there, listening. And I said, "Hey Pastor, how are you doing, it's Kate; I'm panicking right now." And he told me to open my bible, so I did. He sent me to Psalms, and I read about David and all the stuff he went through. He said, "Call me back if you don't feel better, because I bet you will." He said, "I'll pray on it."

I called him back to tell him that I felt better and we started talking about Hunter because I had taken Hunter and his two daughters to church with me. I said, "We've decided to move in together; he's going to move in with me." Pastor Angelo replied, "What?" And I answered nervously, "Well, yeah. He has a house he's been trying to sell, and I'm much closer to his work, and it's a huge house. Pastor Angelo stopped me in my tracks and blurted out, "That's—you're disgusting in the eyes of the Lord. You're disgusting." I almost dropped the phone. I thought, "Oh my God, he just used the word disgusting." He could have softened it and said, "You know, maybe that's not such a good idea. You're raw, why don't you give it some time?" He just called it out like that. I said, "Really? Really? Pastor, I have to go." And I hung up. I never heard from him again. I stopped attending his church and have not heard or seen Pastor Angelo to this day.

I stood there in the kitchen, and Liz said, "What did he say to you? Your face is white." I said, "He just told me I was disgusting." Liz looked at me and fire was in her eyes as she replied, "Screw him, Kate. Screw that judgmental hypocrite! She just went on and on, and I said, "You're right." I said, "He's just a man. The bible tells us we're not supposed to judge each other. There's only one person we have to answer to, God himself." And I thought, "He's breaking his own rules. It's so hypocritical." I felt angry, and thought, "You know what, I'm happy and Jack needs a male figure in his life. My family is not here. I've got no one, but I've got Hunter. Hunter showed up; he was willing to stand by me and hold my hand." I was telling myself, "How could that be bad? How is that bad?"

Samantha and Martin sent a whole series of letters, maybe nine or ten altogether. The first and second letters were hand written. The third letter was from an attorney.

The fourth letter, which I received in November and after I saw the Nyad interview, was filled with vile and false accusations about me.

It all started with the first letter when Martin asked me for the information on the life insurance policies. I gave Martin all the information: Steve's social security number, the phone number to call, whom to ask for, Steve's date of birth, his middle name, everything they needed to find out who the beneficiary was, or was not. I was assuming that Samantha was the beneficiary.

The next correspondence I had with Martin was after they discovered that Samantha was not the beneficiary of the life insurance policy Steve owned.

I responded to his letter by email: "Martin, I'm really sorry that you and Samantha have found yourselves in financial duress; that's not my fault. All the choices that you made regarding your car, quitting your job, etc., were on you." I also said, "I'm not going to give you $170,000, but here's the deal, I will help you. I want to help you." This is what they didn't know; I was willing to help them for the rest of their lives. Anybody that knows me knows that I'm the most generous person in the world. I love to give; it's my love language. In June, I offered to give them $10,000 to help with the birth of the baby, due in October.

Martin responded coldly, saying the offer of $10,000 was a slap in the face. In one of his letters, Martin accused me of infidelity. He assumed I knew Hunter all along, throughout my whole relationship with Steve, and he accused me of hurting the entire family. He said that I was an evil person and that I hurt everyone. I believe he was attempting to scare me into giving him some money.

Steve died on April 6th, the funeral was on April 10th, and I met Hunter for the first time on April 18th. I don't know how Martin and Samantha even knew that Hunter existed, maybe from Facebook or something. But Martin accused me of having known him for much longer than I did. He also said that he couldn't have a relationship with Jack; it just ripped my heart out when he said that because that little boy idolized them. Not only did Jack lose his father, he lost an entire family!

Jack had gotten to know Samantha and Martin. He would call Samantha "Sissy." Steve died in April, Jack's birthday was in May. He said, "Are Sissy and Martin coming to my birthday party, Mama?" They didn't even send a card, let alone show up. They said it was too painful for them to be around Jack since all I cared about was money. That spoke volumes about their character.

I responded the very next day to Martin's horrible accusations and continued requests for an astronomical amount of money. I stated with conviction, "A husband's job is to provide and protect. You and Samantha are not my responsibility or Steve's. The minute she married you, she became your responsibility. This is biblical. Please stop trying to leech off another man's life for your livelihood. Steve paid for her wedding, her college, and other things. I wish you all the best. Do not contact me again.

ALMOST SHATTERED

The minute you cut Jack out, you said everything. That speaks volumes of your true character. God Bless, Kate."

Martin's greed concerning money was one thing, but his cruelty toward Jack was something else. When a mother's child, the love of her life, is threatened, she becomes a lioness. You forget yourself, and you will do anything to protect your child. I felt like a soldier preparing for battle. A true warrior ready to defend myself and my boy at any given moment!

I received a letter from Mr. Deveroux, Esq. Samantha and Martin's attorney, asking me for a copy of Steve's will....This was laughable because any attorney knows that a will is public knowledge. He could have looked it up himself or sent a clerk to retrieve it. I got the will and had my lawyer, Robert Banks, send a copy to him. Robert said again, "Kate, don't lose sleep over this." Robert claimed that this was basically extortion and blackmail and that Samantha and Martin were trying to bully me into giving them money.

The first letter from Mr. Deveroux, Esq. was followed by another one a couple of months later. This letter was addressed to my lawyer, and my lawyer forwarded it to me. It said that Martin and Samantha wanted $170,000. He accused me of infidelity, undue influence, and withholding food from Steve as well as verbal abuse and threatening divorce—some pretty horrible things. This guy thought that he knew everything about everything. He said, "As you know, Mr. Banks (to my lawyer), Samantha and her father were in very good standing." Well, that's not true. They weren't in good standing, at all. Samantha filled this guy's head with what she wanted him to believe; she played innocent and put on her little girl voice. She was a master at manipulation and persuasion. I had seen her in action many times using her whiles on her own father.

Samantha was a great actress, but I saw through her immediately. And even though I was freaked out about the awful accusations the attorney was throwing at me, I was not letting it ruin my life. It was shocking and traumatizing to see those words on paper, but I didn't write the check. I told my attorney, "Well, let's go to war then. Let's do this because I'll appear in front of any judge. So will Steve's doctors, and so will all the people who were there every day. Martin and Samantha don't have a chance." Robert said, "You're right, they don't." I kept thinking, "I'm going to trust in the Lord. I'm going to trust God because I'm standing in truth. I will find a way. No matter what happens, Jack and I will be fine. What do I have to do to manage this? I thought about my feelings, the threats, the pending threats, and being taken to court and accused publicly.

It was in October that Martin contacted me again via text. He texted me and said, "Hey, we've had the baby. I'd really love to come over and have you meet Quinn. You could play with the baby, and we could chat." I responded, "I would love to meet you and the baby. I'd like to give you a gift, and I'd like us to start over. I'd really love to start over. I love you and Samantha, and I always have. Can we just start over?" Martin flatly replied, "No." When he said, "No, that's not possible," I knew. I thought, "The only reason he's contacting me is because he still wants money." He wanted to talk with me and use the baby as a pawn. So, I blocked his number so I wouldn't ever hear from him again.

It was a crisp fall day, and Jack was at his swim lesson with Grace and I was with Liz at the mall. I wanted to do something fun. I asked Liz to do some Christmas shopping with me. I was having a great day, laughing, talking and shopping when my phone rang. It was Hunter calling. His voice was calm and even when he spoke. He proceeded to tell me that Martin just paid a visit to our house. I nearly dropped the phone. I exclaimed, "What?" Hunter continued to relay the story to me in detail.

Hunter was the only person at home. I was at the mall about 45 minutes away and was headed back when Hunter called and said, "Guess who just stopped by?" I had no idea who it could have been. Then Hunter said, "I had just gotten out of the shower when I heard the doorbell ring. I looked through the window and saw this awkward looking, hipster type kid at the door. I figured it was Martin. I told him nicely to leave. The boy kept trying to get into the house. I blocked the entrance with my body. I raised my voice and told him emphatically to leave the premises and never return, ever. I also suggested he get a job and take care of his family like a real man." Hunter told me Martin kept saying, "I need to talk to Kate, I have to talk to her. It's about family stuff. Please let me talk to her, please." He was begging. And Hunter replied, "No. Leave. You are not welcome here after what you accused her of, just go." Martin said, "Please, please, please, you don't understand."

"He appeared desperate," Hunter said. Because he knew he wasn't going to get any money, they were going to try to woo me with the newborn baby." Hunter told Martin, "If you ever come back here, it will be very bad for you." He asked Martin not to return. He didn't hit him. He didn't punch him. He didn't call him horrible names. He just said, "Leave." I thought that he practiced a lot of restraint. Since that November, we have not heard from Samantha and Martin once.

December 3rd, 2014, brought a final challenge. I opened my email to find a message from nobody@disom. com, sent from some obscure site. He did not give his name but said that he was a friend of the Williams family and had known Steve for years. He went on to say, "I'd like to offer my condolences. Grief is such an unexplained pain and can cause us to do and say things to hurt other people." He went on for a while, and then he said, "The main concern for me writing to you is that I have had conversations with Steve in the past about securing a future for his kids." He told me that he had seen Samantha over Thanksgiving and wanted me to consider and have compassion towards her and give her money...." (Yep!)

He said, "My name is not important." and "I have debated reaching out to you as it seems it would be best not to give my input on the circumstances following Steve's death. The emotional turmoil that I have heard from the Williams family, whom I've been close to since Steve and I were younger, made me reach out to you."

It seemed to me that Samantha and Martin wanted his help in getting some money from me. He was embarrassed enough to not even put his name on the email; he just wanted to say something but not be involved.

Now, I had the strength to respond to this anonymous harasser in my own defense and tell the truth.

I said, "Dear friend of Steve, if you are close to Steve, you know two things for certain about my late husband. One, he was very, very intelligent. Two, he never, ever did anything he did not want to do. Knowing this, you realize everything that happened after he died was planned except that his family would cut Jack and me off like a dead appendage. I offered Samantha and Martin $10,000 to cover the medical expenses of having a child. Martin told me this was a slap in the face. I cried. While my husband was ill, I begged Samantha, Martin, Marion and Johnathan to come visit, have dinner, and see Steve. Samantha and Martin said, 'They were too busy and could only do what they could do." Marion and Johnathan came to our home two times in seven years. Steve and I traveled at least four times a year to Kansas. And regarding your letter, this family broke my son's heart. Not only did he lose a father, he lost an entire family, and he is devastated."

"I was left, devastated and alone with a five-year-old. No one offered to stay with me, comfort me, grab a coffee with me or make sure I ate. They just didn't care. You stated in your letter that I should have compassion for Samantha; compassion is defined as 'a feeling of wanting to help someone in struggle.' It is also defined as 'sympathetic consciousness of other's distress.' I have shown compassion to Samantha and Martin, in spite of the letters and the accusations that I received in June. Can you imagine my emotional pain? I loved Steve deeply. I fought for his dignity every day and worked with all the sleep studies, the machines, the insurance companies—I dressed him, I shaved him, I groomed him, I fed him, I went to every doctor's appointment. I have a binder two inches thick with my notes about his disease. I took his blood pressure and pulse every day. Martin contacted me several weeks ago; I asked if we could start over. He replied, "Samantha is too hurt right now, but I'd still like to meet with you."'

I went on to tell this anonymous emailer what happened with Martin. I explained that I offered him money and he said it was a slap in the face. I also told Mr. Anonymous that I asked Martin if we could start over, and he said no. I shared how much I have tried to mend the relationship with honesty and love. I said, "All of this has caused tremendous turmoil in my life. I loved both of them very much, and they walked out of Jack's and my life. I hope you understand why I have no desire to associate with them. They hurt my boy. Nobody has the right to destroy a little boy's heart. It also confused him greatly. Samantha broke her father's heart when she never came around. Steve was disappointed time after time because of her lack of attention and caring. Whoever you are, I was Steve's wife. I loved him more than you could possibly imagine. Do not contact me again! Regards, Kate."

I never heard from that person again, whoever he was. I view my ability to respond to him as I did as a sign of growth and increased confidence. My journey has been difficult, at times impossible, but I found a way to handle the pain. I grabbed each obstacle and smashed it into pieces. My experience changed me, forever.

CHAPTER 8

Picking Up the Pieces

Steve requested in his will to be cremated. I honored his wishes, every one of them. The owner of the funeral home told me he could keep the ashes in the urn I bought for one year. I was grateful that I had time to process the thought of scattering his remains. April 6th (one year later) was around the corner. I had received a few emails from Mr. Trannino regarding Steve's ashes. He wanted to know when I was planning to come and retrieve them. I emailed him back and asked for some more time. He said, "Certainly, but not too much longer, Kate. You really need to deal with this." I knew I had to go and pick up the urn and confront my fear. I asked Jules, Liz and Hunter to accompany me to the funeral home one day in May. They all agreed to come with me for support.

The day we decided to drive to the funeral home and retrieve the ashes was beautiful, warm and sunny. Steve adored the mountains and asked to be scattered somewhere peaceful among them. We all agreed to get the urn and drive up into the mountains to honor Steve's final request. I'll never forget the feeling of walking into the funeral home and seeing Mr. Trannino. He was so robotic and monotone. I don't think I ever witnessed him smiling! He looked at me and said, "Hello, Kate, nice to see you today." Ughhhh, he was so strange! He honestly had zero expression on his face. I politely and quietly said, "Hi, what's next?" He casually replied, "I'll go grab the urn for you, Kate." I stood there waiting. While we waited, I thought "Oh my God, help me! I'm going to have to carry what's left of my husband away in an urn." How does one do this with poise and grace? I tried. I tried very hard to not emote. I kept it together until I got back to my car, then I lost it! The tears streamed down my face, and my hands were shaking violently. Jules offered to drive. I let her. As we drove up the mountain looking for the perfect spot, I cried more. We finally found the perfect place! There was a beautiful stream bubbling over some pretty rocks and foliage. We parked the car, and I bravely held the urn and walked down the hill to the stream. I opened the urn, pulled out the sack of remains, opened it gently and let his remains spill out into the stream. I remember when I first saw the contents of the sack. Oh my God, it was so painful! I let out a guttural scream and heard myself saying over and over, "I'm sorry honey, I'm so very sorry." It was traumatic and cathartic, simultaneously. We were all crying when we decided to rise and leave the spot by the stream. It was over. I just witnessed what was left of my husband float away down the beautiful stream of water. As the remains, which resembled sand, floated away, I screamed, "I'm sorry honey, I tried...I really tried." I rose slowly from my knees and thought I was going to pass out. The world looked surreal all over again. It's as if this final act made everything real. He wasn't coming back. Steve was gone, forever. I think one of the worst things a human will ever have to do is see the remains of their lover, best friend and husband pour out of a sack.

The first three years of our marriage were bliss. No one was sick, we had a lovely home, good jobs and a perfect baby boy. Life was good; it was easy. We traveled a lot, and both Steve and I loved to travel. I remember feeling so "normal." For the first time in my life, I felt like the average, American housewife and mother. I enjoyed blending in and NOT being in the spot light. I liked that there was very little drama and lots of love and laughter....

Steve fell ill three years into our marriage. The dynamic of husband and wife quickly changed to caregiver and sick person. I was the primary caregiver, and Steve was the sick person. He needed me, relied on me and clung to me at times. I never thought in a million years, my husband would be diagnosed with a fatal illness. It's like one minute we're planning our retirement, and the next minute we're planning an end of life celebration. It happened that fast. Steve's illness was like a black cloud that followed us everywhere we went. There was no escape, no reprieve. It was always there to remind us. I heard it

163

all from friends and family, "Life is short," "You will be a widow eventually" and the most gut wrenching sentiment, "Jack is going to lose his dad." These reminders were constant and ever present.

The reminders today are everywhere as well. I'll hear a song, smell a familiar scent or stumble upon an old photograph. The memories are bittersweet. I miss the normalcy, the routine and the feeling of security I had being married to Steve. I never worried about finances. I trusted my husband to provide for Jack and me, and he always did. He was always so agreeable to most of my ideas. I know I gave him the best years of my life. I was loyal, kind and a warrior for him when he fell ill. I did the very best I could with the situation I was handed. Most folks forget after a while about your troubles. They see you out, working, living and think everything is peachy, she's fine now. No one realizes the pain is ever present. You learn how to live with the pain, manage it, minimize it, feel it and move through it as gracefully as possible.

Death, sickness and loss make most people uncomfortable. They don't want to hear about it, see it or (God forbid) experience it! When you are going through something that feels completely surreal and strange, it's hard for others to relate. I always put my game face on and battle. One thing I've learned for sure over the past three years is that one must fight. You can never give up or surrender to the enemy. Fighting back is the only option

I had. Of course, the other option for me was death. I always kept it as an actual viable alternative. Why? I have no idea. Especially when I know suicide is a permanent solution to a temporary problem. Because of the Lord, Jack and my dear friends, I have not entertained checking out for good in many years. Today, I face every problem, every obstacle and every moment with God by my side. I've been through my worst nightmare, so life's little inconveniences don't throw me anymore. It's a gift you get from becoming a survivor. You learn to appreciate life and all its little blessings. Every day that I wake up is a good day. Every day that Jack is happy and healthy is a victory. I have pursued my dreams and goals with a voracious appetite for success. Looking back is not option. I remember the story of Abraham and his nephew Lot. God chose to save Lot's wife from death and destruction, and the only thing the Lord asked her to do was, "do not look back…" She did. Now she's a pillar of salt. The moral of that story is "stuff" is just "stuff." It can all be replaced. Human lives cannot. So, don't look back, focus on the future and of course, the present.

I've heard it said many times, "When you have one foot in the future and one foot in the past, you are pissing on today!" Wow, how true is that? It's so true!! I try to stay in the moment, every moment. I ended up pulling Jack from the "so-called" Christian academy and put him in the local grade school. The teachers and principal of that academy picked on Jack. He actually received

ALMOST SHATTERED

a "hair violation"!!! Can you imagine? My little, golden,
five-year-old boy with gorgeous, curly hair got in trouble
because some of his locks touched his collar. Well, stop
the presses and call the law! I was blown away by the
audacity of the school to chastise my son for his nat-
urally beautiful hair. Sorry if I didn't have time to take
my son to the barber while my husband was dying and
being memorialized. The hair violation was simply the
last straw! I marched into the main office of the school
the next day and asked for my boy's things. They had
everything ready for me. The snooty receptionist looked
at me with her big, judgmental eyes and said, "Oh, here
you go… that's Jack Williams, right?" Wow! She had his
books and school supplies ready for pick up! I swear the
women I met at that school were like Stepford Wives.
All the moms talked about was baking cookies and pee-
wee baseball and soccer, etc.…. God forbid they share a
feeling or share something of significance. I could not,
for the life of me, play their stupid, phony games. Especially after everything I was going through! I wanted
real, warm, down to earth women to talk with and share
thoughts and feelings. So, I pulled Jack out of the nightmare school and put him in the local public school in
our area. The first time I walked into the new school, I
knew instantly it was awesome. Everyone smiled and
said hello or bye-bye. It was very refreshing. It took Jack
about a week to adjust to his new school, but he finally
did. I hated to leave him there, crying his eyes out every

166

time I dropped him off. I had to walk away. All my wise girlfriends told me, "The best thing you can do for Jack is to let him figure it out." I did just that. I let my little boy figure it out. After a week or two, he was smiling and saying, "Bye Mom! I love you!" What a relief to see Jack smile again. I knew I had made the correct decision to switch schools.

The days seemed to pile on top of one another. Before I knew it, one year had passed. Soon enough, two years had passed. I still receive mail for Steve. I have never heard one peep from his family other than a letter from an attorney explaining Steve's mother, Doris, had passed away. I received the letter three months after she died. The family didn't give me a chance to send flowers, write a letter or attend the services. They kept me as far away as possible for reasons I will never know.

Betrayal, I have heard, is worse than rape. Being betrayed hurts on so many levels of your psyche. You experience loneliness, doubt, anger and rage. All I wanted was for the pain to stop. Each day, it got a little easier. The friends that turned away, the community that turned a blind eye and a deaf ear, the family that tried to blackmail me and of course the loan shark who threatened myself and my son; I survived it all. Minute by minute, hour by hour and yes, day by day I crawled through the minutes, hours and days until it was over. The dust has settled. Do I think of Steve? Yes, at times but not nearly as much as I used to think of him. Does Jack ever ask about his dad?

No, he does not. Does Jack ever ask about the family who left us behind? Thankfully, never! Do I cry about Steve's death? On occasion, of course, I do. Do I cry for Jack? Yes, all the time. My heart breaks for my son that he had to endure losing his father at age 5. I can't change this fact. I can only control my response to what happens to me. This lesson was probably the biggest and most profound. When I finally actually realized that I couldn't control Steve's illness or pain or suffering, I found peace. There is a certain peace that follows acceptance and release. I carry that peace with me to this day.

I realize now ever so clearly that life is short. I am a widow and my boy, Jack, lost his Dad when he was only five years old. We survived the worst. Jack and I are still standing. I'll never know why Steve hid things from me. I'll never know why the Christian school and my church disappeared when my husband died. I will certainly never know why the people I called my family for seven years betrayed me brutally. Perhaps, I may never know the answers to any of these questions. It doesn't matter. The bottom line is that Jack and I are ok today. We survived death, betrayal and abandonment together. We grew closer as mother and son and stronger as individuals because of this horrendous ordeal. God never left us, and those who showed up in the worst of times are still in our lives. Those who chose not to show up, are not in our lives in any capacity. The saying, "You find out who your true friends are when the going gets tough" is absolutely true. Jack and I talk about Steve from time to time, but Jack doesn't ask a million questions anymore! He rarely asks about anyone in Steve's family. We take one day at a time and some days, one hour at a time.

Life can change so quickly! In a heartbeat, life can be forever altered, and you will never be the same. What will you do? How will you respond? The only thing we can control is our response to what happens to us! Learn to breathe deep, stretch, take a walk and listen to your loved ones when they speak to you. It may be the last chance you have to hear their voice! Above all else, love. Love strong, love deep and love unabashedly! Be shameless! Be spontaneous! Be you!! It's so very important to enjoy life. If you feel sad, find out why! If you're miserable in your job, get a new one! Fear can paralyze and retard. Look fear in the face and move through it! Courage is not, not being scared. True courage is being scared and doing it anyway! Life is not an emergency. I learned this the hard way. When Steve was diagnosed, when he fell ill, and when he died, I thought I'd never survive. Breaking down the hours into moments one day at a time helped. All we have is today. Live it boldly.

CHAPTER 9

Lessons Learned

Life as I knew it would never be the same. If you have ever lost someone you loved dearly, you know that the feelings can be gut wrenching, heart breaking and devastating. I am a believer in Jesus Christ. The one comfort I carried with me was knowing Steve, also a believer, was in a much better place, heaven. I pictured him healed and happy. I envisioned him chatting with Peter, Paul and John. I imagined he saw Jesus and cried tears of pure joy. These thoughts kept me sane.

Steve wanted to be cremated. He wanted his Memorial service to be short and meaningful. I did that for him. I honored his every request. I remained kind to his family even when they hurt me. I prayed for Steve's family daily, hoping to neutralize my feelings of anger. I continued to take care of Jack, to the best of my ability. I paid bills, went to work and cooked dinner every night. I pushed myself through the pain and muck of intense grief. God held my hand, and when I was too weak to move, he moved me. He carried me through every thought, every attack and every uncovered revelation. My Redeemer lives. There is no question and no doubt.

Looking back on what I survived, I feel grateful. I was tested and passed the test. I was pushed, shoved and stepped on but remained faithful to my Almighty. The battle was His ultimately, not mine. I saw through, with sheer transparency, my true friends vs. the imposters. God gave me that gift. Not many of us really know which relationships are based in love vs. relationships based in selfishness. I am forever changed.

Today, I have confidence, strength and gratitude. I live life intentionally with purpose and do not take my loved ones for granted. Knowing life is so short, I appreciate the beauty around me. If you read this book and now have hope, my journey was worth the pain. If you think that you too can survive the impossible, you can. There is no doubt in my mind that when we ask God for help, He helps. Grief, loss, death and divorce can be paralyzing. Look up from your knees, and let the Lord inside your broken heart. God hears every critical cry, every plea for help and every desperate call. He hears it all.

EPILOGUE

Happily Never After...
More Lessons Learned

Hunter Ridge was not an answer to a prayer or my happy ending. Hunter was a man, just a man. He happened to be the first man I met immediately after my husband died. I met Hunter exactly 12 days after the death of my husband. I wasn't ok. I certainly wasn't in a place to make any life-altering decisions. When Hunter moved in with me and sold his house, I thought things would be great. I thought there was so much fire and love, we would be fine. I was wrong. I was very wrong. Hunter chose me. The night we met, I was out with my girlfriends, drinking because of my birthday celebration. I told him that night that I was newly widowed and had come into some money. Between the cocktails and that I hadn't danced with a man in years, I'm sure I appeared pretty ripe for the picking! Hunter was the typical "bad boy" women like me fall for. I was always attracted to bad boys. It seemed counter intuitive to what I should be attracted to and that was all part of the fascination. Hunter was sleeved with tattoos on both arms. He was dark and swarthy. His lips were luscious and full (almost like a woman's deliciously pouty mouth). His eyes were nearly jet black, and the curve of his face suggested he had lived through much pain and pleasure. Hunter had a dark side that was scary and sexy at the same time. He took me places sexually I had never been. Capture, manipulate, control and enslave was his modus operandi. He, for lack of a better way to describe, made me his emotional and psychological slave. He knew exactly how to play me. He was the musician, and I, the instrument.

I remember the first time in our courtship that I felt true, to the core, fear. I had come home from the gym and was feeling up and positive. Liz was there organizing the kitchen cabinets (as she often did) and being her vivacious self. I was headed toward the fridge to grab a cold drink, and Hunter suddenly appeared in the entrance and said, "What's your schedule today?" I was immediately taken aback and could feel my pulse quicken and adrenaline rush. I looked right at him and said as casually as I could muster, "Oh, just some errands and stuff like that." He looked at me intensely. The mood in the room shifted from light and hopeful to dark and uneasy. He quickly replied, "What errands?" I started to feel like I was being observed under a microscope. Why did he care what, where or who about my day??? Was it any of his business, anyway? He's never asked before what I was doing all day. It was the way he asked me that struck me as odd. I couldn't hide my exasperation. I stumbled through my words answering, "I don't know, pick up Jack from school, go to Target, stuff like that." Then I committed the ultimate sin and asked, "WHY?" He went on an hour tirade about me acting funny and "offish" when he inquired about my day. He said I appeared nervous like I was hiding something. He only asked, he says, because he wanted to know if he and I could spend some time together during the day. I'm thinking, "What in the world is wrong with this man? He's weird and creepy!" He sat on my bed, practically in tears, saying how much he needed me. He actually said, "I just need YOU, all of YOU."

The days went on from there, pretty much the same way. I'd get up bright and hopeful and dread the moment when I'd hear his footsteps. A rush of relief would wash over me when I'd hear his diesel engine pulling out of the driveway. The days when he'd stay in bed all morning were the most frustrating. My father and Steve NEVER lounged around unless it was a Saturday morning!! Hunter would say, "I am working, getting paid right now baby." This meant that some other "hand," as he referred to them, was on a job site making Hunter money. To this day, I'll never understand how a grown man can justify staying home doing nothing." I could never do it myself, as much as I'd try!

I remember that the bathroom became my sanctuary. It was the only place I could justify to Hunter being alone for a few minutes. I'd hide my phone under my blouse and text Jules. I'd tell her how crazy he was and how scared I felt. There was a distinct feeling of being trapped like a bird in a cage or some zoo animal. I couldn't make a move without him watching me. I never knew but for months he had been reading my emails and my texts. I'm positive he read my journal as well, even though I hid it in different places. Emotionally, I was raw. I could not handle another loss. I kept hoping against all hope the situation with him and me would improve. I tried everything from crying to expressing my undying love and at times showing anger. It's like it was impossible for him to show empathy or compassion. I began to feel guilty about missing Steve and needing to talk about things. I slowly began to pull away from Hunter in every way.

As I grew stronger with each passing day, Hunter's mood swings, temper and affect got worse. It's like he was afraid I'd one day wake up and say," Oh, by the way, I'm good now, you can leave." I wanted things to work out. I wanted our relationship to blossom and flourish. On one particular morning after a year of being together, I had to train a client at my gym. I was getting ready for work and applying some makeup. Hunter sat on the edge of the tub and watched me. He simply sat there and stared at me. My hands noticeably began to shake and tremble. I couldn't put eyeliner on because my hands were so unsteady. I looked at him and said, "What are you doing? Going to work today?" He looked at me as if I'd asked him to cut off his right arm. "Why?" he retorted gruffly. "Why do you want to know?" I, trying to calm my nerves and remain nonchalant about everything, answered, "Oh, I was just wondering, no reason." His eyes bore holes through me. I continued with my morning routine as best I could and was finally ready to leave the house. I went to him and kissed him on the cheek and said, "Have a great a day sweetheart, I'm off to the gym." He paused, then said," I don't feel well, I think I'm having a heart attack." I was shocked. As a trainer and athletic coach, I know the signs of someone experiencing cardiac arrest. I asked him with true empathy, "Is your heart beating rapidly? Are you experiencing a pain running from your right arm to your chest? Are you having difficulty breathing? And lastly, does it feel like there is an elephant sitting on your chest?" He looked at me strangely and replied, "No" to all the above. So, I mustered some courage and said, "Well, I don't think you're having a heart attack, I think it may be some anxiety. However, I am not a doctor and if it's that uncomfortable, you ought to go see a doctor or pay a visit to the local emergency room." I then walked away and headed to my car. I told him flatly, "I have to leave for work." He started crying like a child. He begged, "Please don't leave me! I'm sick, I swear, baby please, I need you." I again repeated calmly and firmly, "I can't help you. If you feel that bad, call a doctor or go to the hospital; I have to go to work." I then got in my car and left for the gym. About one hour into a training session with a client, Hunter texted me and said he was moving out. He was very upset and angry with me for not taking him to the hospital myself. He told me I was an awful person. I remember reading the text and thinking, "This guy is absolutely crazy town! What a nut job!" After work, I drove over to the local ER. I found him sitting upright in his hospital bed and gown texting on his phone. The doctor told me there was nothing wrong with Hunter and that his EKG was perfectly normal. I greeted Hunter with a casual but friendly, "Hello, how are you feeling?" He looked at me and said, "Why do you care?" Oh boy, here we go, I thought. I'm surely in for another hour or more speech on my lack of compassion. That's exactly what happened when we both arrived home.

The days were like this for the next year. I'd get stronger and start smiling and laughing, and Hunter would find something wrong with my behavior. I was never with him enough or touching him enough or having sex with him enough. Everything was my fault, and he was a victim. I didn't know this at the time, but Hunter was a narcissist and true sociopath. The last nine months of our relationship were hell. He became abusive verbally, financially and mentally. He stayed out till all hours of the night and never called. One night I thought he died in a car wreck. I called his family, hospitals, the police and my best friend. I was beside myself with worry and anxiety. He finally arrived home 48 hours later. He looked at me after he stepped out of his car and said, "What's wrong, baby?" I nearly dropped to the ground with a heart attack! What's wrong, he asked?!!! I slowly and calmly answered, "You have been gone for almost two days. I thought you were dead." He replied casually, "Baby, it was very bad weather. I slid off the road into a ditch and spent the night in my car." I did not believe a word he said. He was fine, the car was fine, no mud no scratches, no nothing. One month later, on my son's 9th birthday, he called me from the exact phone he said he "dropped" in the snow. Hunter Ridge was a pathological liar. My plan was to buy tickets to Texas and get the hell out of dodge. I did just that! I bought Jack, Amy and myself one-way tickets to Houston, Texas. We would stay with my mom until Hunter was gone forever. I needed desperately to feel safe. The night before our trip, Hunter never came home. I was relieved. I had a great time with my family and really dreaded returning to Colorado to face the music. On the flight home from Houston, I was sitting in an aisle seat. We were about one hour into the flight when a woman across from me named, Karen, tapped me on the shoulder. She said coyly," Are you an author or composer?" I was stunned. How did she know? I replied, "I sure am! I'm both." She continued to tell me she was moved to speak to me by the Holy Spirit. I felt a sense of calm come over me when speaking to her. I ended up spilling the whole Hunter saga. She paused and asked, "Have you invited the Lord into the situation?" I thought for a moment about the question she posed. I had prayed. I had cried. But had I really invited God in? The answer was, "no." I thanked her for her words of wisdom, and we exchanged business cards. When I got home, I fell to my knees and invited God into this unholy mess.

Hunter was not there when we returned from the airport. He showed up about 30 minutes after our arrival at the house. God, he frightened me. I looked at him and saw a gargoyle. I saw an ugly, twisted beast of a man before me. The truth was evident. I avoided touching him in any way and said I was exhausted.... He pouted and threw a tantrum as usual and finally left the room. I fell asleep and prayed God would fix this, somehow. The next morning, Hunter was gone. Around noon, two police officers appeared at my door and explained Hunter had been arrested and charged with multiple felonies. He had been stealing cars, motorcycles and anything else he could steal for drug money. Hunter had been using a drug called meth. I was in a daze. I truly didn't see drugs. I saw craziness, mood swings and anger, but I never thought he was using drugs. I had been blinded. Things started to make sense and fall into place. The disappearing, the stealing of my credit cards, my jewelry and ultimately my life. I remembered the awful night Hunter grabbed me and squeezed me so tightly I had bruises all over my arms, I should have known then that he was on something!

Anyway, it was done. The truth was revealed, he was in prison, and I was free. How I allowed this to happen, I will never know. I know now that I was raw, fragile and in no position to be in a relationship with anyone after Steve died. It was the loneliness, the fear, the ache for human touch that drew me to Hunter. My flesh was crying out, and my spirit was dormant when I met the devil himself. Oh, how the enemy has tried to take me out. Using my own vulnerability as a weapon against me. Wow! He's clever and may have won a battle, but he will never win the war. I am free now. Free and joyful! I love my son and my career and my amazing friends. I have learned so many tough lessons. The ultimate lesson I need to remember always is, trust God, trust my gut and listen to those around me who truly care.

People will tell you everything you need to know by their actions and body language. Hunter's actions were simple to observe. He did nothing. He did not work. He did not help me with Jack or the household. He contributed zero financially. These observations told me what I needed to know. It was I who was in denial. I didn't think I could handle another hit, loss or defeat. I told a doctor friend of mine, "I am delaying the pain." I called it pain procrastination back then. However, once I invited God into the situation, Hunter was removed from my life, immediately. I will forever be grateful for the woman on the plane who had the courage to listen to the Holy Spirit and tap me on the shoulder. My gratitude for my friends goes without saying. They carried me. They know who they are. Life continues, and I am free. I will wait on the Lord to bring me my next partner. God will choose, and I will listen. Amen.

Made in the USA
Las Vegas, NV
17 November 2021

34662967R00101